REBELLIONS IN CANADA

DESMOND MORTON

FOCUS ON CANADIAN HISTORY SERIES

Grolier Limited
TORONTO

Dedicated to Ed and Lucille Broadbent
and to all who share their conviction
that justice and equality can come to
Canada only through democratic struggle.

Cover: The capture of Batoche, May 12, 1885

Cover Design and Maps: Didier Fiszel

*Selected Further Reading courtesy Maureen Kaukinen, East York
Board of Education*

Illustration credits: Public Archives of Canada, cover and
pages 14, 21, 23, 29, 36, 48, 50, 67, 73, 80, 84, 87, 89;
Ontario Archives, page 41; Glenbow Alberta Institute, page 55;
the Hudson's Bay Company, page 60; Saskatchewan Archives
Board, pages 78, 85.

Canadian Cataloguing in Publication Data

Morton, Desmond, 1937-
Rebellions in Canada

(Focus on Canadian history series)

Includes index.
ISBN 0-7172-1800-7
ISBN 0-7172-1806-6 (pa.)

1. Canada—History—Rebellion, 1837-1838. 2. Red
River Rebellion, 1869-1870. 3. Riel Rebellion, 1885.
I. Title. II. Series.

FC162.M67   971   C79-094691-2
F1033.M67

3o,8 l 9

4567890   MP   987654321

Printed and Bound in Canada

Contents

Preface

Why should we study our rebel ancestors?

There are many good reasons. If we can understand why Papineau, Mackenzie and Riel became so angry at the governments of their own time, we may learn how frustrations can build to boiling point in our own day. We will see that unfair systems of government, even when they are supported by most people in the community, drive desperate men and women to violence.

In our own day, native land claims, the struggles of working people inside and outside unions, and the continuing friction between French and English in Canada all reflect issues raised by Canadian rebels more than a hundred years ago.

We should be very careful not to see rebellions as a struggle of heroes and villains. Such judgments are too simple. At the time, the rebels of 1837-8, of 1870 and 1885 were bitterly condemned by most Canadians. Today, rebel leaders like Mackenzie and Riel have become national heroes.

This kind of history teaches us nothing. We should draw on the past for experience, not try to make it a simple battle of good and evil. Rebellions reflect a clash of ideas and values. The Métis, the *patriotes* and Mackenzie's Reformers, whom you will meet in this book, had a strong case. So did the Montreal merchants, the Family Compact in Upper Canada, the Canadians at the Red River and the Macdonald government in Ottawa. Only when we try to bring both sides together can we grow in understanding our country and ourselves.

This book would never have been written without the relentless encouragement of Ken Pearson of Grolier. It would never have reached its final state without the devoted work of Barbara Hodes and Kathy Jourdain. Without the good-natured persistence of Clara Stewart and Doris Olsen of Erindale College, too many academic obscurities would have survived. To them and to my long-suffering family belongs the credit; the author dutifully assumes the responsibility. Few of my undertakings have proved more challenging or more satisfying.

Introduction

Most of us have been rebels at one time or another. Perhaps we rebelled when we felt that we had been unfairly treated, or when we had a goal we wanted to accomplish and someone stood in our way. At first we probably tried to get someone to listen to our complaints and help us solve our problem peacefully. But if this did not work, we were likely to become so angry that we just went ahead and tried to get what we wanted however we could. Perhaps we were later punished for our "rebellion" but maybe we also finally were able to get someone to listen to our complaints.

Throughout history rebellions have happened in all countries. When a rebellion accomplishes what it sets out to do, we call it a revolution. A revolution is a complete and often violent overthrow of the established government. For example, in France, the Revolution of 1789 ended the power of kings and led to the rule of the people, which we call democracy. The Russian Revolution of 1917 overthrew the emperor, called a czar, and ended in the establishment of a new form of government called communism.

In Canada, there has never been a revolution, but there have been several rebellions in which a minority of people have given up trying to solve their problems peacefully and have turned to violence. A recent example is the "October Crisis" of 1970, when a small group of French Canadians kidnapped a British diplomat and a Quebec politician and threatened to start a revolution to overthrow the government if their demands were not met. Although it is extremely unlikely that such a small group would have been able to carry out this threat, the federal government called on our armed forces to help the police hunt the would-be rebels.

Canada has also known other, far more serious rebellions. In 1837, rebels in Upper and Lower Canada (now Ontario and Quebec) collected guns, practised military manoeuvres and set out to overthrow the government. In 1869 and again in 1885, the Métis people, who were part French Canadian and part Indian, proclaimed their own government in western Canada and tried to stop the Canadian government from taking over their land. Both times they failed.

Why would people risk their lives in a rebellion? Obviously they must have serious complaints or grievances against the established government, and they must see no peaceful way of solving their problems. After all, we hear complaints every day about the government. We read them in the newspaper and we hear them from politicians, but few people ever talk seriously about starting a rebellion. Instead, they plan to make their dissatisfactions heard by voting out the government in the next election. This opportunity to express our unhappiness with the government is what makes ours a democratic system.

Rebellions are caused by the frustration of unsettled grievances, but one more thing is needed before a rebellion can start. Rebels need a leader who is able to draw out the support of the people and organize them to act in defiance of the law. When we look at the four important Canadian rebellions, the rebellion of Lower Canada, the rebellion of Upper Canada, the Red River Rebellion and the Northwest Rebellion, we may understand why their supporters decided to attack the government, even at the risk of their lives. However, we must also ask another question: Why did such leaders as Papineau, Mackenzie and Riel find so few faithful followers in spite of their justifiable complaints about the government and their promises to better the lives of the people after the government was overthrown? We will discover the answer to these questions when we look at each rebellion in turn.

For the time being we should remember that although these rebellions may have failed at the time, over the years many of their goals were met, and unpopular parties and groups were eventually removed from office. So while the rebels were not able to get enough people to support them in action, their ideas still had a deep and lasting effect on the course of Canadian history.

LOWER CANADA 1791-1841
*The Constitutional Act of 1791
divided the original province
of Quebec into two provinces,
Lower Canada and Upper Canada.*

The Rebellion in Lower Canada

The motto of Quebec is *Je me souviens,* which in English means "I remember."

Among the memories of French Canadians is the rebellion of 1837, waged by their ancestors who tried in vain to establish their own country on the banks of the St. Lawrence River. For some, that rebellion remains unfinished; even today they still want an independent Quebec. Others believe that this rebellion was a mistake. They argue that history later proved that more could be accomplished by compromise and peaceful discussion.

The Papineau Rebellion of 1837 was not just an uprising of the people against a government they considered unfair. It was the result of the unhappiness of a conquered race, the French Canadians, who felt a strong call to preserve their identity, which they felt was threatened by the domination of the British. As Lord Durham, who was sent by the British government to investigate and recommend solutions to the problems in Canada, said in 1838: "I expected to find a contest between a government and a people: I found two nations warring in the bosom of a single state."

Many blame the British for what happened in 1837. After the conquest of New France in 1760, French Canada became part of the British Empire. The British respected the law, the language and the religion of their new territory. In 1791, the new, mostly French-speaking colony of Lower Canada had an elected Legislative Assembly. In return for the respect shown to them, the French Canadians, including later rebel leader Louis-Joseph

11

Papineau, helped the British fight American invaders in 1776 and again during the War of 1812.

However, the British made serious mistakes when it came to governing what is now Quebec. Their governors were mainly former soldiers: stubborn, proud and sometimes suspicious of their French-speaking subjects. Any real power was with the Executive Council of senior, mainly British officials, and with the Legislative Council, an upper chamber of members appointed by the governor, not with the elected Assembly. Whatever the Assembly said or did could be ignored by the governor and his powerful advisors. Angry critics called these people the Chateau Clique, because they spent so much time in the governor's residence, the Chateau St-Louis.

If the British had had to deal only with the French Canadians, their problems would have been smaller. However, they also had to cope with a growing number of English-speaking people who moved to Quebec after the Conquest. First came the merchants, eager to become rich by taking over the fur trade in the interior. After the American Revolution of 1776, a host of Americans loyal to the British arrived to demand land and justice under the British flag. Together these two groups gained control of the wealth of the province through their domination of both business and the banks.

After 1815, the fur trade that had enriched Montreal for a century and a half would never again be profitable. Control of it had gone to the Americans and the Hudson's Bay Company. Montreal merchants had to find new ways to make money. They saw they could do this by supplying Britain with wheat and timber. Once, French-Canadian farmers along the St. Lawrence and Richelieu Rivers could have supplied the wheat, but now their soil was exhausted and their crops spoiled by wheat fly. They could grow only oats and rye and big granaries in towns such as St. Denis near Montreal stood empty. The Montreal merchants had to find their wheat in Upper Canada or in the American states along the Great Lakes. There was one catch: to bring wheat down the St. Lawrence River meant building big costly canals. Only the Assembly could raise taxes to pay for these canals, but the French-Canadian members refused to vote in favor of these taxes. Why should they help the English settlers of Upper Canada?

In 1815, Louis-Joseph Papineau was chosen Speaker of the Assembly. A well-educated man, he was a quick-witted, powerful and spell-binding speaker. He was a natural leader for the French Canadians who controlled the Assembly. He was also an inspiration to an important group in the colony, the educated young graduates of the Catholic colleges. Although the majority of French Canadians were uneducated farmers, called *habitants*, there was an elite core of educated young men who found it difficult to find positions that suited their backgrounds. Many became priests, but those with other ambitions were frustrated. Business was dominated by the British, and efforts to become government officials were hindered by the Chateau Clique, which kept important jobs for its supporters. When Papineau demanded the right to control government spending through the Assembly, he was really demanding the power to give government jobs to educated young French Canadians.

This meant little to the *habitants*, struggling desperately to make a living and finding it more difficult year after year. Much of the fault for their condition lay with primitive farming methods and Lower Canada's traditional seigniorial system under which farmers, *habitants*, were tenants who tended the land of the owners, called *seigniors*. But the *habitants* blamed the British and the arrogant Montreal merchants, not their landlords, for their troubles. Men like Papineau, who owned seigniories, naturally preferred not to be accused of neglecting their own people.

Was there nothing to be done about the discontent of Lower Canada? The Montreal merchants had an answer. In 1822, they asked Britain to unite Upper and Lower Canada. Then, they thought, an English majority would agree to build canals and scrap old-fashioned French laws. Papineau was shocked, and he responded by taking a protest petition to London, where he was successful in persuading the British Parliament to abandon the idea of union for a time.

But time only made grievances more bitter. Educated

Lower Canadians looked elsewhere for answers. In 1828, the Americans chose Andrew Jackson as their president, and it looked as though the common people of the United States had won a great victory against their bankers and rich merchants. In 1830, the King of France fled for his life as Paris burst into new revolution.\The move for parliamentary reform in England had resulted in the Reform Bill of 1832, which challenged that country's aristocratic government. Papineau's followers were encouraged by these examples of the victory of democracy, although so far the British government had offered only concessions that seemed to the *patriotes*, as Papineau and his friends were called, to be too little too late. In 1834, an angry Assembly listed its long-standing grievances, large and small, in ninety-two resolutions. Until the complaints were met, Papineau's support-

Louis-Joseph Papineau was an eloquent, emotional speaker and a skilled politician.

ers insisted, they would vote that no taxes be collected from the people.

This was no idle threat. Government officials could not collect their salaries. The building of roads and bridges stopped. Papineau went further and ordered the *patriotes* to attack the English merchants "in their dearest parts—their pockets." Denis Viger started a Bank of the People. Some supporters whispered that its real purpose was to collect money for the purpose of buying guns for a revolution that, by 1835, was already talked of in Lower Canada.

Was revolution what Papineau really wanted? After 1834, old allies such as John Neilson and Elzéar Bédard, who had written the Ninety-Two Resolutions, began to disagree with some of Papineau's stands. They did not like his attacks on the Catholic Church, which he hated for its loyalty to the British. Yet in spite of his fiery speeches, Papineau still clung to many of the old institutions of French Canada, particularly the seigniorial system. It is fair to say that many of Papineau's supporters were far more radical than he was. They wanted a revolution that would destroy the traditional, old-fashioned Quebec their leader loved. Papineau hoped that his threats, like his mass meetings and a campaign against buying British goods, would frighten the British into making concessions.

If Papineau's *patriotes* talked increasingly of violent revolution, it was partly because they had more and more grievances against the aggressive merchants of Montreal. Frustrated by Britain's refusal to unite the two provinces in 1822, and by the Assembly's control of taxes, the merchants had decided that the only answer was to swamp the French-speaking majority by immigration of English-speaking people. The big, leaky ships of the timber trade came back to Quebec from Britain jammed with immigrants. Many newcomers went to Upper Canada or to the United States but some stayed in Lower Canada. London and Montreal merchants obtained a huge land grant of 800,000 acres in what is now the Eastern Townships along the United States border. This area soon became populated with English-speaking farmers.

Immigration became a bitter complaint among the *habitants*. Where would their sons find land if the English took it all? How could they sell their produce when the newcomers sold their crops at lower prices? In 1832, an immigrant ship brought the horrible disease of cholera. It swept across the Canadas in the most deadly epidemic anyone could remember. Not only did the English "cast their beggars on the Canadian shore," raged one of the *patriotes*, "they must do still more; they must send us, as the final outrage, pestilence and death."

In 1835, the British government tried to calm Lower Canada by sending out a new governor, Lord Gosford, with special orders to investigate all the grievances in the Ninety-Two Resolutions. Lord Gosford was a cheerful, easygoing Irishman who was quite unlike his stuffy military predecessors. However, he had no power to remedy grievances on his own. Soon the Montreal merchants hated him for his efforts to please the *patriotes* , while Papineau despised the new governor as a puppet of the British.

As if Gosford did not have enough problems, crops failed in Lower Canada and across much of North America in 1836. The governor immediately ordered supplies from the United States and Britain, but shipments were slow, prices were high and many people faced starvation. Discontent among French Canadians was reaching the boiling point. In January, 1837, Gosford sent a report on conditions in Lower Canada to London. Finally, on March 6, the British government gave its reply. Ten resolutions passed by Parliament destroyed any hope of compromise. The Assembly in Lower Canada was denied more power. British immigration would continue to be encouraged. Above all, if the Assembly refused to vote to levy taxes, the governor would have power to take from the treasury the money needed to pay officials.

Papineau had hoped that the British would make enough concessions to save him from having to lead his followers to outright revolt. The ten resolutions forced him to action. The *patriotes* formed a permanent central committee. Its members sat late into the night, arguing and dreaming about a new Republic of

Lower Canada. Younger members formed the Sons of Liberty to train for the coming fight. As their "general", the Sons chose Thomas Brown, a bankrupt hardware dealer. At St. Denis on the Richelieu River, a hotbed of anger at British rule, the leader was Wolfred Nelson, a country doctor who had served as an army surgeon for the British in the War of 1812.

That year, 1837, brought disaster to the Montreal merchants. A terrible economic depression occurred in the United States and Britain; prices tumbled and many businesses failed. "In my day," wrote the president of the Bank of Montreal, "such times have never been experienced." Even the rich Canadian timber trade collapsed. The anger of the merchants was directed at the French Canadians. Lord Gosford banned a British rifle corps set up by the merchants' sons, but he could not stop their organizing Doric clubs to fight the Sons of Liberty in the streets of Montreal.

In August of 1837, Lord Gosford summoned the Assembly for one last vain try to stop a rebellion. Papineau was resolute. Nothing but a "popular and responsible government" was acceptable. On August 26, Gosford dismissed the Assembly. Lower Canada was in turmoil. Villages chose committees of public safety, imitating the actions of the French Revolution, which had started in 1789. Gangs of men, faces blackened, attacked Loyalists, burning barns, smashing houses, cutting off horses' tails and manes so that the poor animals were driven mad by flies. As a result of these actions, loyal officials packed up their families and possessions and fled to Montreal, while others resigned their positions.

A few tried to stop the rush to rebellion. Bishop Joseph Lartigue of Montreal told his priests that rebellion was never permissible. He issued a stern letter to be read from every pulpit: the government must be obeyed. Papineau himself pleaded for patience. He commanded his followers to organize larger meetings so that the British would be impressed by the size of the unrest. "The democratic flood has poured irresistibly down the slope of time," he told them. Why turn to violence when the people would soon win without it?

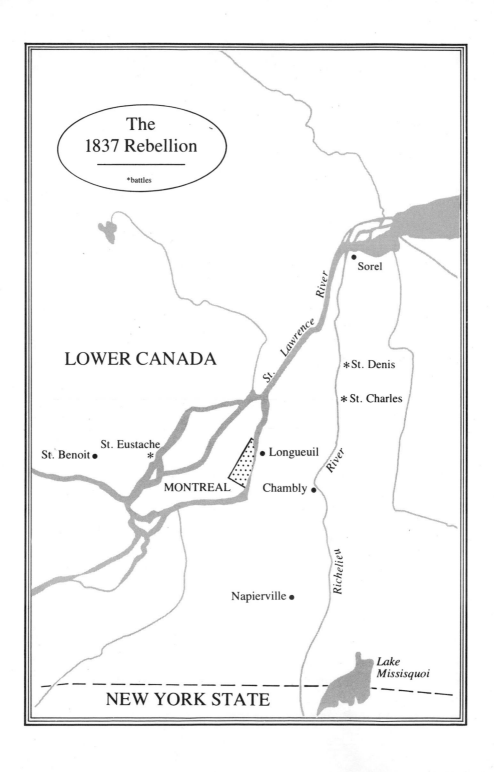

The
1837 Rebellion

*battles

Sorel

LOWER CANADA

*St. Denis

*St. Charles

St. Benoit ● St. Eustache * ● Longueuil

MONTREAL Chambly ●

Napierville ●

Richelieu River

St. Lawrence River

Lake Missisquoi

NEW YORK STATE

The Fighting Begins

Did people understand that Papineau wanted to compromise? Or did they listen to other, angrier voices? At St. Charles near Montreal on October 24, 1837, thousands of people streamed down wet, muddy roads and over sodden fields to hear their leader. Papineau pleaded for more time, hoping that the threat of revolt could still pressure the British into meeting his demands. Wolfred Nelson cried: "The time has come to melt our spoons into bullets!" That was the voice the audience had come to hear.

If it was war the British wanted, they at least had a strong leader. Sir John Colborne, one of Britain's best officers, had come from Upper Canada to command the garrison. However, fighting would not start between the British redcoated soldiers and *habitants* in open conflict, but in the narrow, dirty streets of Montreal, between the two factions, the Dorics and the Sons of Liberty. On November 6, a foolish brawl grew in minutes into a pitched battle. Houses of *patriote* supporters were wrecked. Papineau's house however was saved by the arrival of British soldiers, who defended it.

Frightened by the violence and by rumors of mass arrests, on the night of November 13, Papineau and his supporter O'Callaghan fled from Montreal to St. Denis. To Gosford and Colborne, the flight could mean only one thing: the rebellion was about to start. On November 16, arrests of the *patriotes* began. The local Doric club was recruited as a volunteer cavalry. A troop set off to St. Johns, deep in *patriote* country, to make arrests. Next day at dusk, near Longueuil, outside Montreal, shots were fired. A crowd attacked the young volunteers and rescued the prisoners. Two men lay wounded. The rebellion had begun.

For all their preparations, the British knew nothing of the rebels' plans. The reason was simple: there were none. For all their blustering and bragging talk, the *patriotes* did not know what to do next. People gathered in their villages all over Lower Canada, but when no encouragement came from their leaders they grew frightened and went home. Only in two areas were things different. The Assembly members for the Two Mountains district west of Montreal, William Scott and Jean-Joseph Girouard, had backed Papineau. People in this region hated the English who lived in settlements to the north and south of them. In the Richelieu Valley, Wolfred Nelson would lead the resistance he had helped to arouse.

The resistance would be weak. Viger's Bank of the People had not purchased the guns they had promised. The villagers had nothing but knives, clubs and a few rusty muskets. At St. Denis, Captain François Jalbert had drilled a company of fusiliers. They were the only *patriotes* who even pretended to be soldiers.

At Montreal, Colborne knew nothing of *patriote* weakness or divisions. He did know that he had very few soldiers and a very hostile countryside. His answer was to strike boldly. The rebels in the Two Mountains district could wait. The worst threat lay in the Richelieu Valley, dangerously close to the United States. There was a danger that American republican sympathy could turn into arms shipments. It was decided that Colonel George Wetherall would march north with 350 men from the British fort at St. Johns to Chambly and that Colonel Charles Gore with 300 men would march south from Sorel.

Soon Colborne had second thoughts. The two British columns were too weak. Gore and Wetherall had to wait to attack. Messengers raced out of Montreal with fresh orders for the colonels. None of them got through. During the night of November 22, Gore and his men marched south. The roads were knee-deep in mud. Again and again their cannon stuck in the rutted track. It was morning when the exhausted, near-frozen soldiers reached St. Denis. The *patriotes* were waiting. Doctor Nelson positioned his men well. Gore's gun made no dent in the stout stone house where the *habitants* sheltered and his weary soldiers made little headway against the rifle fire. When the redcoats faltered, the *patriotes* took heart again and hundreds of supporters came in from the countryside to join the fight. Hungry, despairing and worn out, Gore and his men fell back, leaving six dead and the cannon behind. The first battle was over and it was a triumph for the *patriotes*.

On the same day, Colonel Wetherall had stopped at St.

*The Highland Light Infantry rounding up prisoners
during the rebellion in Lower Canada.*

Hilaire. News of Gore's defeat made him wait a second day. No orders came. At dawn on November 23, Wetherall marched on St. Charles. Here the *patriote* leaders were Bonaventure Viger, who foolishly set his men building a wood and mud wall as a defence, and Thomas Brown, who was caught trying to flee, as had several rebel supporters. When Wetherall's soldiers emerged from the woods, it took only a few minutes for his guns to pulverize the mud wall. The British troops swept forward, bayonets flashing. For all their desperate courage, the *habitants* could not win. That evening, the British found sixty rebel bodies on the field. Next day, Wetherall's men and thirty prisoners marched back to Montreal.

The defeat crushed the *patriotes*. On November 30, Colonel Gore returned to St. Denis. He found only a few men flying a white flag of surrender. Soldiers fanned out through the little town, ransacking houses, blowing up the stone house that had earlier defied their cannon and leaving fifty homes blazing. At St. Charles they burned more homes. St. Hyacinthe met them with priests and citizens and delayed Gore's men long enough to allow Papineau to escape from his sister's house, where he had taken refuge after fleeing the first attack on St. Denis.

On their way back, the soldiers learned the fate of one of Colborne's messengers. Half-buried under the ice at St. Denis lay the mutilated body of Lieutenant George "Jock" Weir. Caught trying to escape from the *patriotes*, Weir had died under the clubs and pitchforks of a furious crowd. Now the soldiers of the British would march to avenge Weir. Some rebel leaders would escape that vengeance. Although Colborne sent volunteer cavalry to patrol the frontier, Papineau, O'Callaghan and a half-dead Thomas Brown escaped to the United States. Others were caught, including Bonaventure Viger, François Jalbert, and Wolfred Nelson.

Deliberately, Colborne had left the rebels at St. Eustache in the Two Mountains district until the rivers and road froze. Caught between the Loyalist Glengarry settlers to the south and English-speaking farmers of St. Andrews, the rebels could do little and they lost heart. Amury Girod, a cowardly Swiss adventurer sent to be their military commander, plotted escape. Only the young local doctor, Jean-Olivier Chénier, and Abbé Etienne Chartier rallied the *habitants* against the coming attack.

By the time Colborne marched out on December 13, most of the rebel leaders had fled. Maxime Globenski, seignior of St. Eustache, led the cavalry well in advance of the marching troops, giving the timid rebels plenty of warning so they could escape.

At dawn on December 14, the soldiers crossed the ice. Chénier rallied his remaining supporters into the stone church and convent that dominated the village square. The troops battered their way into houses. A few Montreal volunteers crawled along the river bank, burst into the church and kicked over a stove, causing the interior to burst into fire. Some of Chénier's men leaped from the burning building while others

The artillery forcing an entrance into the rebel-occupied church of St. Eustache, December 14, 1837.

perished in the flames. Chénier himself was killed outside. Some who tried to surrender were shot down by soldiers shouting "Remember Jock Weir."

Next day, Colborne marched to St. Benoit. Terrified villagers helped the British search out guns, ammunition and rebel fugitives. Next morning, the British soldiers marched away, leaving behind two thousand farmers from St. Andrews and other English settlements to guard the village. These volunteers looted and burned St. Benoit.

Previously, on November 19, Lord Gosford had had a caller, Louis-Hippolyte LaFontaine, one of Papineau's radical young supporters. LaFontaine had an astonishing message: "Papineau is lost and must be sacrificed." Call the Assembly, he urged, and compromise would still be possible. It was, Gosford suggested sadly, too late. Yet somehow peace had to be made. Lower Canada could not forever be governed by Colborne's bayonets.

News of the rebellion hit Britain like a thunderbolt, as the trouble-ridden government there had paid little attention to the situation in its distant colony. Lord Melbourne, the British prime minister, appointed John George Lambton, Earl of Durham, to straighten out the conflict. Lord Durham was an enemy of Melbourne's because he had forced the government to carry out radical reforms. Melbourne thought that the political situation in Lower Canada was hopeless and that he was getting rid of a potential rival for government office by sending Durham to Canada. Durham was one of England's richest and most snobbish aristocrats. Though he was in bad health, he was too proud to refuse the post of governor general of Canada.

Lord Durham Arrives

Long, cruel months passed before Durham could arrive in Canada. The prisons were full of rebels. No trials took place because Colborne knew that no French-Canadian jury would convict the rebels. Indeed, opinion in Lower Canada was swinging sharply from anger at the rebellion to sympathy with the rebels. Even moderate French Canadians were horrified by the burning and looting, the mistreatment of rebel prisoners and the arrogance of the triumphant English. This mood encouraged the growing number of exiled rebels now in the United States. So did support from Americans who saw the rebellion as a further stage of their own revolution. Papineau was welcomed as a hero in the United States and went to Washington to obtain aid for further rebel activities. He returned empty-handed: the United States was determined to stay out of the quarrel.

Papineau soon faced another setback. His *patriote* followers were more radical than ever. New leaders such as Wolfred Nelson's brother Robert, a doctor from Montreal, called for abolition of the seigniorial system, with its feudal customs. On February 28, 1838, Robert Nelson proclaimed himself president of the new republic of Lower Canada. The only result was more arrests in Montreal.

On May 27, Lord Durham finally arrived in Canada. To the French Canadians he meant little. To the English merchants, he brought his reputation as a dangerous radical, one of the authors of the Reform Bill of 1832. Their fears seemed well-founded. Durham immediately dismissed Colborne's Executive Council and broke up the Chateau Clique. Prison conditions improved. Generals and magistrates began visiting the more important prisoners and listening to their complaints.

Durham could not bring peace to Lower Canada while the *patriote* leaders were still in jail. Since no jury would convict them, they must be persuaded to confess to their crimes. By June 14, Durham had heard long statements from Wolfred Nelson and seven others. Ten days later, the new governor general set most of the other prisoners free and exiled eight leaders to Bermuda. Papineau and others who had fled to the United States were to be executed if they tried to return to Canada.

Montreal merchants responded with rage to this judgment, while French Canadians felt their first surge of hope. That hope was misplaced. Durham deserved his nickname of Radical Jack. He despised the self-seeking Chateau Clique, but he also rejected the old-fashioned mixture of racial, religious and rural values that were the basis of French-Canadian society. In fact, Durham admired only one group in Lower Canada — the Montreal merchants. Only they, he thought, had aggressive, imaginative plans for the Canadas. Far from sympathizing with the *patriotes*, Durham condemned Papineau and the Assembly majority for obstructing the economic progress of Lower Canada.

South of the border, Robert Nelson and his friends began to plot and organize. American sympathizers started a new organization, the Hunters' Lodges, to help the Canadians. Called the *Frères Chasseurs* in French, the organization filtered into Lower Canada. Rumors spread that a Republican Bank of Canada had set out to raise $7 million to buy guns, thinking war was imminent between Britain and the United States. In London, Durham's enemies pointed out that the governor general had no authority over Bermuda. His banishment order was illegal. Lord Melbourne agreed. Lord Durham was frustrated by the lack of

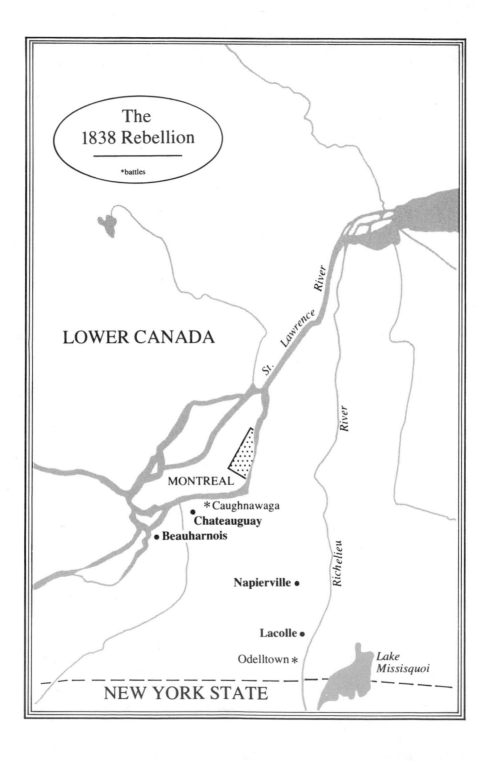

support he received from London. Worn out, sick and humiliated, Durham had only one answer. He would resign and return to England. On November 1, his ship left Quebec. Sir John Colborne and his advisors were back. Within two days, a new rebellion broke out.

Most of the rebel rumors were unfounded. Few volunteers came. The Republican Bank of Canada had gathered a mere $300. The United States government was as determined as ever not to become involved. When Robert Nelson landed on the banks of the Richelieu River just north of the border, his supporters did not know that his American supporters had gifted him with 250 rifles, $20,000 and one undersized cannon which represented his full resources. Twenty miles away at Napierville, Dr. Cyrille Coté used the *Chasseurs* network to collect three thousand men. Five hundred more gathered at Beauharnois and hundreds at Chateauguay.

Colborne was on his way to Montreal when he heard the news. His plans had been made long before. All summer men in the English settlements along the border had been armed and drilled. Within hours of the invasion, they were marching. From Upper Canada, a thousand Glengarry men set off. Near Napierville, Coté's men ran into the volunteers and left eleven dead. Their leader fled to the United States and Nelson commanded the sorry remnant to march to Lacolle. Morale sank still lower when Nelson himself tried to escape and was brought back under guard.

On November 9, the desperate, leaderless rebels ran into more volunteers at Odelltown. Both sides fought hard and at first the outnumbered English farmers gave way. Then, when more men arrived to help, the volunteers counterattacked. Out of hope and ammunition, the *patriotes* fled for the American border.

Farther west, the *patriotes* at Chateauguay and Beauharnois waited for orders. Some went off to seize arms from the Iroquois at Caughnawaga. The Indians were waiting for them. In a brief fight, the *patriotes* were seized and sent as prisoners to Montreal. On November 9, men from Beauharnois surprised and defeated a little column of British soldiers but the victory came too late.

Clouds of smoke on the horizon showed that the Glengarry men were coming. By the next morning, the rebels had scattered to save their lives.

Within a week, the rebellion of 1838 had collapsed. Columns of British soldiers, volunteers, and Indians marched down the Richelieu Valley. Behind them, smoke and flames rose from the farms of suspected rebels. To the west, the Glengarry men boasted that they had left a trail of destruction six miles wide. What they missed coming they would get on the way home. Lord Durham, the soldiers coldly noted, had not killed rebellion with kindness. They would do it with fire.

In Montreal, three makeshift prisons were filled with suspects. Every day, columns of cold, ragged prisoners marched in from the country. Outside the prisons, carpenters hammered together a set of gallows. This time there would be no worry about juries. Power now lay with military courts. On December 21, two of the men taken at Caughnawaga were the first to be executed. On January 18, 1839, five more rebels were hanged for murder and rebellion. When Colborne's court martial of the rebels ended on May 6, 1839, it had tried 108 men, convicted 98 and hanged 12 of them. The appetite for vengeance was satisfied. The remaining twelve hundred prisoners were set free. Mostly, it was not leaders but followers who suffered the gallows. To French Canadians, the fate of 58 more, sentenced to the distant penal colonies in Australia, seemed even more horrible.

Was harshness a better cure for rebellion than Durham's tolerance? Rumors of risings and invasions continued, but now there was no substance to them. The *patriote* exiles turned to fighting with each other. Elbowed aside by his former followers, Papineau had set off for Paris, where he aroused little interest or sympathy. Even American supporters grew tired of the *patriote* cause. Soon the French Canadians wanted only to go home to Canada.

To French Canada, rebellion had brought every disaster that Papineau could have feared. Lord Durham's report, written in England during the last months of his life, advocated the union of Upper and Lower Canada, killing the hopes for a separate

most members of the Assembly or it must be changed. Could such a radical system work in a colony? Durham thought so. Britain would continue to control important areas such as defence and foreign relations, but the colony would be self-governing in other areas.

In Britain and in Canada, the idea of responsible government took time to be understood. Papineau had issued the words with a different meaning. So had his Upper Canadian counterpart, William Lyon Mackenzie. By responsible government Papineau and Mackenzie simply meant good government. As the years went by, the memories of their speeches about government faded. In 1845, LaFontaine won permission for Papineau to return from exile.

By 1847, both Papineau and Wolfred Nelson were members of the new Assembly. But the 1840s belonged to new men and new ideas. Governors were forced to accept the power of an elected Assembly in the new united province of the Canadas. LaFontaine used his power to find official positions for the well-educated malcontents who had been so dangerous in 1837 and 1838. Once in office, they soon forgot their radical ideas. In 1849, he also used his power to force through a Rebellion Losses Bill to repay those who had been victims of burning and looting by Colborne's men. Even some of the rebels received compensation for the damage done to their homes by the British soldiers.

Again there was talk of rebellion, but this time by the outraged English merchants. They were opposed to and horrified by the idea that those who rebelled against the government were to receive compensation for their losses. The governor general was attacked in his carriage and the Parliament buildings in Montreal were burned by a furious mob of Englishmen. This time it was the merchants who drafted protest resolutions and called for annexation to the United States. In fact, however, both sides had learned a lesson. Rebellions demand a high price of those who make them and those who oppose them.

The Rebellion in Upper Canada

It was a cold, gray December morning in 1837 when the messenger came to Sir John Colborne, commander of the British forces in Canada. A rebel band was marching on Toronto, left defenceless by the departure of every British soldier to Montreal to stop the rebellion in Lower Canada. Now, the province of Upper Canada too was in revolt.

Although the rebels in both provinces shared some of the same ideas, such as that too much power was held by only a few officials, and that an American-style republic should replace the colonial system of government, the two rebellions had little in common. They were as different as the two men who led them.

Louis-Joseph Papineau looked back proudly to more than a hundred years of Canadian ancestry. He was a rich, well-born man who kept his distance from the ordinary people. William Lyon Mackenzie, on the other hand, came to Upper Canada in 1820, a widow's son with hardly a penny to his name. He believed himself the equal of any man and resented the snobbery of the British and Loyalist establishment who looked down their noses at a poor Scottish immigrant. A man whose temperament was as fiery as his red wig, Mackenzie was self-educated and in his early years in Canada worked as a druggist, bookseller and newspaper publisher. By 1824, he was married, prosperous and voicing his many opinions through editorials in his newspaper, the *Colonial Advocate*, started in that year.

In close touch with the settlers in the area around Queenston where he lived, he became sympathetic to their grievances against the colonial government in York (now Toronto) and began to ask embarrassing and difficult questions of this government, such as, why had veterans of the War of 1812 waited so long for free land when they had been promised it? Where were the roads and bridges and schools the settlers had been promised? Why did the government charge $2.50 an acre in Upper Canada when land was so cheap in the United States? Why had one-seventh of all the good land in Upper Canada been kept as Clergy Reserves supposedly for the benefit of all the Protestant churches, but in fact exclusively for the Church of England. These uncleared reserves cut off pioneer farmers from their neighbors and blocked expansion by the more prosperous among them.

Inflamed with a passion for justice, Mackenzie launched a furious attack on government officials and their influential supporters. In 1824, he moved his family and his newspaper to York, where his outspokenness and radicalism won him few friends among the Family Compact, the elite group that ruled the government. Like the Chateau Clique in Lower Canada, members of the Family Compact were wealthy, conservative and strongly pro-British.

According to the law of the time, both Upper and Lower Canada were governed by colonial governors who came from Britain and were appointed by the Queen. When the colonial governors arrived in Canada, they knew few people, but were acquainted with the names of certain wealthy, Church of England families. These families exerted great influence on the governors who otherwise knew little of the hearts and minds of Canadians. In Upper Canada members of these families, or the Family Compact, won jobs for themselves and their friends in the government, and soon powerfully influenced it.

Archdeacon John Strachan of York, an Anglican, who had mustered the province's pro-British sentiments to help defeat the Americans in 1812, was a key man in the Family Compact; he and his followers felt they had a right and a responsibility to govern Upper Canada as they saw fit. This meant a favored position for the Church of England, a powerful land-owning class

similar to the British aristocracy, and a series of economic decisions that, while they enriched the province as a whole, also lined the pockets of businessmen who supported the Family Compact. The founding of the Bank of Upper Canada in 1821 and the Canada Company in 1823 and the construction of the Welland Canal in 1824 all led to increased prosperity and growth. The population of Upper Canada by 1830 had swelled to four times that of 1812. But the old questions about why the government did nothing to help ordinary settlers remained unanswered.

Mackenzie's persistent attacks on the greed and self-interest of the government, and his strong desire for a government more representative of the people, aroused the anger of his enemies. After he failed in an attempt to get government printing contracts, Mackenzie stepped up his criticism and raked up old political scandals. The elders of the Family Compact grumbled and their young followers decided to teach the red-wigged Scot a lesson. On June 8, 1825, fifteen young men marched into Mackenzie's house where he printed the *Colonial Advocate*, seized his press and threw it into the harbor. All at once, Mackenzie became a hero. The young men were tried, convicted and ordered to pay the publisher $2,450. With the money, Mackenzie paid his debts and bought a new press. He boasted of his triumph. In his newspaper, more grievances and scandals were dragged into the open. More allies and more enemies were made.

Among the angriest people in Upper Canada were the American-born settlers. Before 1812, American frontiersmen had been the most welcome and successful pioneers in the colony. After the War of 1812, their situation changed. Too many American-born settlers had gone back to old allegiances during the war. Under the Alien Law, people from the United States had to live for seven years in Upper Canada and become British subjects before they could own land. At least half the people of Upper Canada were former Americans. To them, the Alien Law was an insult. In January, 1826, a protest committee was formed, with Mackenzie as its secretary. Within days, more than 15,000 signatures successfully backed a petition asking the British government to cancel the law.

Another grievance took longer to settle. Favoritism toward the Anglican church was unpopular among immigrant settlers, many of whom were Methodist, Presbyterian or Catholic. Non-Anglicans were angry at laws that said only Anglican clergy could perform marriages, and people feared that Archdeacon Strachan would take the money from the Clergy Reserves to support only Anglican churches. The Methodists were lucky to find a powerful leader in Egerton Ryerson. As the son of Loyalist parents, no one could call him a traitor to British values. Unlike Mackenzie, Ryerson was cool and reasonable as a debater. Between them, Ryerson and Mackenzie made religious rights an issue in Upper Canada.

Mackenzie decided to become a candidate for the Legislative Assembly in the election of 1828. Unlike most candidates at the time, who offered promises, bribes and cheap whisky, Mackenzie had a different strategy. He published the votes of politicians on 108 different questions. His evidence was damning. According to Mackenzie's "black book," the Family Compact majority had wasted money and trampled on the rights of Upper Canadians. The voters agreed and the Reformers, Mackenzie among them, swept the election.

The farmers and small merchants of Upper Canada expected great things of their new Assembly but they were disappointed. The leading Reformers, John Rolph and Robert Baldwin, had few new ideas. The shrewdest politician, Marshall Spring Bidwell, was chosen Speaker of the Assembly and in this position he had to be fair to both sides. Most of the new members were poorly educated and had little influence; Mackenzie, however, was a notable exception. He chaired committees, worked tirelessly on problems brought to him by his York County voters, spoke on every issue and drove himself into a state of exhaustion. Often he came home late at night only to face still more hours of newspaper work. Slowly and bitterly he came to realize that it was all a wasted effort. Like Papineau in Lower Canada, Mackenzie learned that a colonial legislature did not control spending. Decisions made by the legislature were overturned by the Executive Council, whose members were appointed by the lieutenant

William Lyon Mackenzie, leader of the 1837 rebellion in Upper Canada.

governor and had no loyalty to the people of the province.

After the first session, a tired Mackenzie made a trip to the United States. He was fascinated by American democracy. No wonder the Family Compact hated the United States, he thought. Here was a country with no aristocracy or overpaid self-serving officials. Mackenzie's admiration for the republican system, which was followed in the United States, was confirmed by what he saw of the bustling prosperity of that country in 1829. However, these pro-American sentiments were out of step with events in Upper Canada, where increased immigration from the British Isles resulted in a renewal of British values, even among Reformers.

In 1828, Ryerson's Methodists broke their links with the American church and forged a connection with the British

Wesleyans. Members of the spreading Orange Order, formed by Irish Protestant immigrants to Canada, were as ready to fight for the British connection in Canada as they had been back in Ireland.

Nor did Mackenzie notice how unpopular the Reform Assembly had become. Upper-Canadian pioneers were glad to have their grievances heard but they also wanted roads, bridges and docks, which the Assembly could not provide because of its inability to control government spending. Also, with the arrival in 1828 of the fair-minded and able Sir John Colborne as lieutenant governor of Upper Canada, the influence of the Family Compact was somewhat lessened and the Anglican church was encouraged to sell off some of the Clergy Reserve land to farmers.

In 1830, Upper Canada's voters gave the Family Compact another chance. Only seventeen of the fifty-four members of the new Assembly were Reformers, but one of them was Mackenzie. For a while, the Tories, as people called the Family Compact supporters, tried a new way of dealing with him. They kept him very busy. He sat on all the committees on currency, roads, prisons, justice, representation and the Welland Canal. In fact, this tactic only gave the angry editor more opportunities to attack the government. The Welland Canal, he reported, was a big waste of money. The currency committee was a platform to attack the Bank of Upper Canada for causing inflation by printing too much money. Mackenzie found a fresh complaint even when the Reformers won a victory. Orders from the British Parliament forced Colborne to get Assembly approval for spending money. There was only one condition. The Assembly must first promise to pay for judges and senior officials. The Tory majority cheerfully agreed. Mackenzie raged at what he called "this Everlasting Salary Bill."

By now, most members of the Assembly were fed up with Mackenzie. They did not like being continually scolded and insulted. On December 12, 1832, they expelled him from the Assembly by a vote of 24 to 15. On January 2, 1833, the voters of York County re-elected Mackenzie and gave him a gold medal for his service. Mackenzie celebrated his victory with a fresh attack on Sir John Colborne. Again he was expelled and, within days, re-elected. Mackenzie's enemies tried other methods. Hired bullies attacked him at Hamilton. On March 23, a mob stormed and ransacked his newspaper office.

New Support

Mackenzie decided to go to England to gain support for his views and to inform the colonial secretary, Lord Goderich, of the grievances of the Reformers. His complaints were given a sympathetic hearing. Lord Goderich agreed that elected members of the Assembly must not be expelled and that the Legislative Council should include other than supporters of the Family Compact. The Family Compact was furious. How dare the colonial secretary listen to such a troublemaker? Lord Goderich's orders, said a Tory newspaper, were "elegant fiddle-faddle." In Mackenzie's absence, the Assembly had again expelled him. Once again, York County voters endorsed their hero. In December, 1833, Mackenzie won his fifth election in two years. Common sense should have told the Tory majority to accept what the York voters wanted, but there was something about Mackenzie that drove his enemies to foolish extremes.

When it was not busy expelling Mackenzie, the Assembly turned to other problems. Muddy York by now was an overgrown village of ten thousand people. It had no sidewalks or lights and there were pigs and garbage in the streets and drunks in the ditches. Only a strong local government could cope with such problems. On March 6, 1834, York became the new city of Toronto. Three weeks later, to the amazement of Tories and Reformers, William Lyon Mackenzie was elected its first mayor.

As usual, Mackenzie worked furiously. In a few weeks, the new administration was organized. When the dreaded cholera outbreak hit Toronto in the summer of 1834, the new mayor helped carry the sick to hospital. However, it was now the Tories' turn to condemn the people in power. They jeered when Mackenzie attacked drunkenness and they sneered when he censored stage shows. Above all, when Mackenzie raised taxes to pay for Toronto's urgently needed police force and sidewalks, the Tories dug out Mackenzie's old speeches against tax increases.

If being mayor were not enough trouble, Mackenzie's bad political judgment got him into fresh difficulties. Mackenzie printed a letter from his radical British supporter, Joseph Hume, which boldly predicted that Upper Canada would soon be free from "the baneful domination" of Great Britain. Probably that was what Mackenzie also hoped, but few in the colony agreed. The letter cost Mackenzie and his fellow Reformers many supporters, including the influential Egerton Ryerson. The Methodist leader was deeply loyal to the British connection. In his new paper, the *Christian Guardian*, Ryerson campaigned against his one-time ally, Mackenzie.

This did not mean that Ryerson and other Upper Canadians turned to the Family Compact. By 1834, such old grievances as the Clergy Reserves, the Welland Canal and the Compact's special privileges had persuaded many voters to give the Reformers a second chance. Once again, William Lyon Mackenzie was elected. This time, a Reform majority would protect him from expulsion. To keep him busy, the new Assembly chose Mackenzie to be chairman of its committee on grievances. Normally, the committee did little. For Mackenzie, it was a chance of a lifetime. Twenty-three witnesses faced his accusing finger, including Bishop Strachan. Mackenzie wrote the *Seventh Report on Grievances*, a five-hundred-page record of almost every complaint, real or fancied, ever uttered by an Upper Canadian. Unfortunately, Mackenzie had no concrete plan of action to correct these grievances, beyond extending more power to the people and less to the Family Compact. Even Mackenzie's fellow Reformers felt a little ashamed of his report. They ordered two thousand copies to be printed but they did not bring it before the Assembly.

One of these copies reached Lord Glenelg, the latest colonial secretary. Like Lord Goderich, Lord Glenelg was surprised by the situation in Upper Canada. Was it true that Upper Canadians were so discontented? Why had Sir John Colborne never told him? The colony obviously needed a new lieutenant governor, younger, not a soldier and, if possible, willing to serve for a lower salary. The choice fell on Sir Francis Bond Head. Only 42, a former army officer who had resigned as a young man to work in Argentina, Head was welcomed by Upper Canada Reformers as a friend and an ally.

Sir Francis Bond Head: A Disappointment

The Reformers were wrong. Sir Francis had no political experience. Like Mackenzie, he was brave, stubborn and conceited. The two instantly became enemies. The new lieutenant governor soon angered most of the Reformers who had welcomed him so warmly. Sir Francis included two leading Reformers, John Rolph and Robert Baldwin, among his official advisors, but when he ignored their advice the two men quit in anger. Their mood spread to the Assembly. The Reformers announced that they would not vote for money bills. Immediately all work on bridges, roads and docks came to a halt. Even the normally cautious Marshall Spring Bidwell caught the mood. As Speaker of the Assembly, he read out a message from Papineau in Lower Canada that practically called for rebellion.

For all his inexperience, Sir Francis Bond Head thought himself a smart politician. The truth was that the Reformers, in their anger, behaved stupidly. They forgot that most people in Upper Canada were as loyal to Britain as was Egerton Ryerson. They also forgot that pioneer farmers needed roads and bridges and would oppose any political efforts to block these. Three weeks after the 1836 session of the legislature ended, Sir Francis called a new election, in which he personally led the Tory forces into the campaign. Never before had a lieutenant governor rushed into a political fight. Handsome, youthful and a good speaker, he delighted audiences. They could vote against their bread and butter if they liked, Sir Francis told his backwoods audiences, but they would know the price. The people, he said, must choose between him and republicanism.

The Reformers had nothing to offer except tired old quarrels. The thousands of newcomers from Britain cared nothing about Clergy Reserves or the wickedness of the Family Com-

Sir Francis Bond Head, lieutenant governor of Upper Canada 1836-1838.

pact. They worried that Reformers such as Mackenzie or Bidwell were too pro-American to be trusted. When the 1836 election was over, Bidwell, Baldwin and most other Reformers had gone down in defeat. Even the loyal voters of York had deserted William Lyon Mackenzie.

Like most losing politicians, the Reformers had a hundred excuses: Sir Francis had used his power unfairly against them; Ryerson had misled the Methodists; gangs of hired bullies had attacked the Reform supporters. In London, Ontario, though, where the worst fights took place, the Reform candidate had won! Most settled down to wait for the next election. A few had had enough. Elections had failed them. It was time for bolder action—time for Mackenzie. Two years before, Mackenzie had

A famous painting of an elderly patriote.

French Canada and ensuring English dominance. Only as a unified country could Canada be prosperous, Durham insisted, and in 1840, the British Parliament approved the union.

Yet constitutions must be supported by people. LaFontaine, who had abandoned Papineau, been spurned by Durham and imprisoned by Colborne, emerged as the new leader of the French Canadians. Clear-eyed, tough, practical, LaFontaine and a new generation of French-Canadian politicians saved their people from the cultural destruction Lord Durham had intended for them. The price was compromise with politicians from Upper Canada and a united fight for responsible government. Responsible government meant that the ministers and senior officials of the colony were to be responsible to the elected Assembly, not to the governor. The government of the colony must be backed by autumn, reports filtered back to Toronto that men were drilling and Sam Lount's blacksmith shop was moulding bullets and forging spearheads. Sir Francis dismissed the reports. He believed Upper Canada was loyal to the core and would not fight. One man disagreed. In his youth, Colonel James Fitzgibbon had been a hero in the War of 1812, capturing an entire regiment of American soldiers. To Sir Francis and his leading officials, Fitzgibbon was merely a tiresome old veteran, and they ignored his warnings. Instead they chose to send British troops stationed in Upper Canada to end the rebellion in Lower Canada.

Although the rebel leaders in Toronto planned to stage only a large peaceful demonstration, which they thought would persuade the Family Compact to surrender its power, their followers outside the city had other, more violent ideas. They insisted the protesters be armed. Anthony Anderson, a popular young farmer, agreed to lead the men. Colonel Anthony Van Egmond of Goderich, a veteran of Napoleon's army, consented to become the rebel general.

"Up, then, Brave Canadians!"

The rebels were shocked into action on October 9 when an exhausted messenger galloped into Toronto with the news that Papineau's *patriotes* were on the verge of action. British troops had left Toronto and thousands of weapons stood unguarded. That night the plotters met at Doel's Brewery. It was time to strike, Mackenzie insisted. With a few men, they could take the guns, seize Sir Francis and proclaim a new government, to be ruled by the constitution Mackenzie had written. His listeners were appalled. They were talkers, not doers. All night they argued and by dawn they had a new plan.

The person who was the key to this new plan was John Rolph. If Mackenzie could bring enough supporters to Toronto to force the government to surrender, Rolph was willing to be president of the new republic. Next morning, Mackenzie rode north with strict orders to collect names of those in favor of the proposed new government. On no account must he talk of armed rebellion. In a week four thousand supporters had signed his petition. Mackenzie had also set a date for the rebellion — December 7, 1837. After another meeting with nervous backers, Mackenzie was off again with new orders. On November 24, he paused at Hogg's Hollow, north of Toronto, to crank out a handbill. Its ringing words were typical of Mackenzie:

CANADIANS! Do you love freedom? I know you do. Do you hate oppression? Who dare deny it? Do you wish perpetual peace and a government founded upon the eternal heaven-born principle of the Lord Jesus Christ — a government bound to enforce the law to do to each other as you would be done by? Then buckle on your armor, and put down the villains who oppress and enslave our country...

"Up, then, brave Canadians!" Mackenzie called. "Get your rifles and make short work of it." As the handbill reached the little towns and villages, word followed of the British defeat at St. Denis in Lower Canada. Would-be rebels took heart.

Slowly the Family Compact stopped sneering and began to make plans. On December 2, Sir Francis summoned supporters to Government House to talk about how to stop the rumors of revolt. Instead, he ordered Mackenzie's arrest and made Fitzgibbon the acting adjutant general. Allan MacNab, a leading young Tory politician and militia colonel, announced that he was going home to Hamilton to prepare his soldiers to fight the rebels.

John Rolph heard the news. The date of the uprising must be moved forward from December 7 to Monday, December 4. Messengers galloped north to find Mackenzie, Lount and Anderson. Before dawn on that cold, rainy Monday, small parties of men trudged through the mud toward the meeting place, Montgomery's Tavern on Yonge Street. They found a poor welcome. Mackenzie was there, beside himself with rage and excitement at the change of plans. The tavern had been sold and the new owner refused to serve food or drink to rebels. Guards were posted and a roadblock built. The rebels tried to keep word of their actions from reaching Toronto; however, Colonel Moodie, a Loyalist veteran, rode south to warn Sir Francis. At the rebel roadblock, he refused to stop. A guard fired. The old soldier tumbled backward from his horse, fatally wounded.

In Toronto, Alderman John Powell stuffed two pistols into his belt and rode north with a friend to learn whether or not the rumors were true. At a rebel post, Mackenzie stopped them, but no true gentleman would search another. Powell's word that he was unarmed was accepted. The two prisoners rode north with Anthony Anderson as escort. Suddenly Powell pulled out a pistol and fired. Anderson fell dead. The alderman wheeled his horse and galloped south. At the Montgomery Tavern roadblock, he aimed his other pistol straight at Mackenzie. The gun misfired but Powell raced through. Exhausted and terrified, Powell hid in the woods until his pursuers gave up. Then he rushed back on foot to Toronto with his news.

When Alderman Powell burst red-faced and panting into the governor's bedroom with his news, the government's overconfidence vanished. The alarm was sounded, but only a few hundred nervous Family Compact supporters appeared. Most of the members of Toronto's two-thousand-man militia paid little attention. Tomorrow was soon enough to join the winning side, they thought.

The panic of the government was balanced by the despair of the rebels. All Monday and early into Tuesday morning, wet, hungry men tramped into the rebel camp at Montgomery's Tavern, where they found confusion, whisky and a hysterical leader. "Little Mac conducted himself like a crazy man all the time we were at Montgomery's," one of them later remembered. Anthony Anderson was dead and Colonel Moodie, a popular, respected old Tory, was dying in an upstairs room. If that were not enough, word of the *patriote* disaster at St. Charles came on Monday evening.

All Monday night and Tuesday morning the remaining leaders argued. Should they give up? Should they wait until Thursday to strike, or attack at once? Finally, Mackenzie took charge. Mounted on a white pony, wrapped in several overcoats to keep off bullets, he called out his men. Then he wheeled and led them, eight-hundred strong, down Yonge Street.

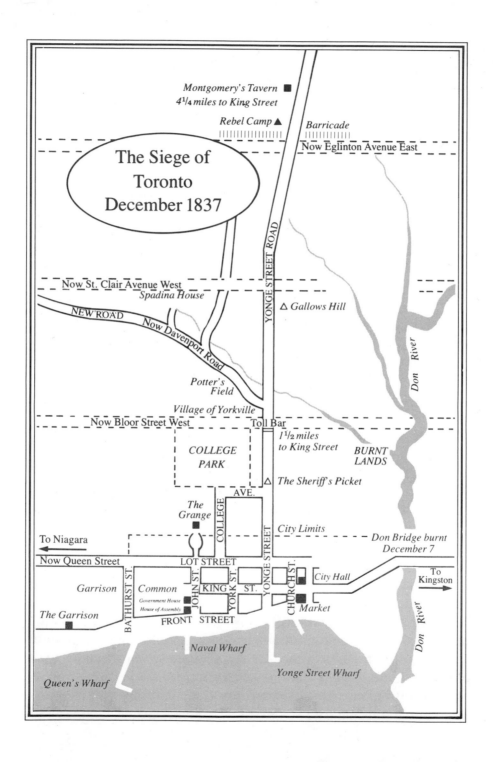

The Siege of Toronto December 1837

Montgomery's Tavern ■
4¼ miles to King Street

Rebel Camp ▲

Barricade

Now Eglinton Avenue East

Now St. Clair Avenue West
Spadina House

NEW ROAD

Now Davenport Road

△ Gallows Hill

YONGE STREET ROAD

Don River

Potter's Field

Village of Yorkville

Now Bloor Street West   Toll Bar

1½ miles to King Street

COLLEGE PARK

BURNT LANDS

△ The Sheriff's Picket

AVE.

The Grange

COLLEGE

City Limits

Don Bridge burnt December 7

To Niagara ←

Now Queen Street   LOT STREET

YONGE STREET

City Hall   To Kingston →

Garrison   Common
Government House
House of Assembly

BATHURST ST.

JOHN ST.

KING   ST.

YORK ST.

CHURCH ST.

Market

The Garrison   FRONT   STREET

Don River

Naval Wharf

Yonge Street Wharf

Queen's Wharf

By early afternoon, the rebels reached the top of Gallows Hill at Yonge and St. Clair. They were an army of solid, honest, ill-educated farmers, equipped with a few muskets and shotguns, pikes, cudgels, and even some carving knives lashed to poles. They stopped while Mackenzie and Lount split them into two columns. Up the hill came two horsemen, John Rolph and Robert Baldwin, sent out by Head to negotiate and to buy time for the government. They succeeded. There was a long delay while the two Reform politicians rode back to get a written promise from Sir Francis that there would be no punishment if the rebels went home. When they came back, Rolph found a chance to whisper the truth to Mackenzie. Toronto was defenceless. The rebels must move.

Mackenzie's followers knew none of that. Instead, they saw Rolph, a trusted leader, acting for the government while Mackenzie behaved like a madman. On the march, he had stopped at the home of a senior official and commanded the official's frightened wife to prepare dinner for his army. Mackenzie smashed down the door of another official's home, killed a dog with a shovel and, when a stove overturned, watched without emotion while the house burned to the ground.

It was almost dark when Mackenzie followed Rolph's advice and started marching. No one noticed Sheriff Jarvis and his men waiting in the bushes just south of present-day Bloor Street. With a flash and a roar, their guns spoke. Then all twenty-seven valiant defenders took to their heels and raced for Toronto. At Lount's command, the leading rebel riflemen threw themselves down and fired back. In the dim light, those behind thought the leading rebels were killed. It was a trap, they thought. Rolph had betrayed them. They turned and fled up Yonge Street. It was their last chance and the rebels had lost it.

By Wednesday morning, December 6, Toronto was safe. Colonel MacNab arrived with fifty men. Colonel Fitzgibbon drilled the militia into order. John Rolph quietly packed his bags and left. On Wednesday night, Sir Francis and his friends met in council of war. Next morning they would attack. At Montgomery's Tavern, the rebels waited. Mackenzie, as frenzied

*The main battle of the rebellion in Upper
Canada was fought near Montgomery's Tavern.*

as ever, robbed a passing mail coach. More men slipped away in
fear or disgust. On Thursday morning, Colonel Van Egmond
arrived. Mackenzie promptly threatened to shoot him when Van
Egmond refused to attack Toronto. After more wasted hours,
Peter Matthews led eighty men to threaten Toronto from the Don
River. Almost at once, word came. The government militia was
advancing.

There was no mistake. With bands and bagpipers, six
hundred militiamen marched up present-day Yonge Street.
Smaller columns moved out on the flanks. South of Davisville
Avenue, Fitzgibbon halted his cannon and opened fire. Van
Egmond had stationed riflemen in the forest south of Eglinton
Avenue. None were hurt by the crashing cannonballs but all were
frightened. From the west, one of the militia columns burst

through the trees. The nearest rebels turned and ran. The guns moved forward to shoot at the tavern. Unarmed rebels spilled out of the building, racing for safety. In half an hour, Mackenzie's followers were running for their lives. Mackenzie was no Papineau. He stayed till the end, screaming at fleeing rebels to fight. The militia was only yards away when Mackenzie fled.

Now was a time for revenge. Mackenzie's rebellion had been a civil war of neighbor against neighbor. Lount, Van Egmond, Matthews and hundreds more were herded into the foul, unheated jails of Upper Canada. In a few days, Van Egmond died. On April 12, despite the pleading of wives and friends, Samuel Lount and Peter Matthews were hanged publicly. Mackenzie would have been hanged too if his enemies had caught him. Sir Francis promised $5,000 for his capture, but Mackenzie successfully escaped to the United States, where he set up a provisional government on Navy Island, in the Niagara River.

The rebellion did not end on December 7. Farther west, another Assembly radical, Dr. Charles Duncombe, gathered a few hundred farmers. They fled when MacNab and his militia approached. Duncombe escaped to the United States, as did other leading Reformers like Marshall Bidwell.

As a refugee, Mackenzie was a hero. American supporters promised money, arms and volunteers. Mackenzie offered excitement and three hundred acres of free land to anyone who would join him. On the night of December 30, a band of Canadian militia crossed the Niagara River and captured and burned the rebel supply ship *Caroline*, killing an American citizen. American anger over the incident caused the United States government to take steps to end rebel activity in that country. Mackenzie was arrested for breaking the law of neutrality between Canada and the United States and was imprisoned for eleven months.

Although Mackenzie returned to Canada in 1849, he was never able to recapture a position of leadership and he retired from politics in 1858. Meanwhile, the recommendations of the Durham Report for responsible government were already far in advance of Mackenzie's own theories on democracy. Responsi-

The fleeing rebels faced a cold and perilous trek across the ice as they sought safety in the United States.

ble government made the colonial government responsible to the wishes of the elected Legislative Assembly on all local matters. This was the moderate compromise that neither Mackenzie nor Papineau could see. While the two rebels endorsed American-style republicanism, Baldwin, Durham and the French-Canadian leader, Louis-Hippolyte LaFontaine, worked out Canada's own form of democracy. Canadians slowly learned to make responsible government work. In 1867, they also learned that power could be efficiently divided between a federal and provincial governments.

Because both Papineau and Mackenzie failed, Canadians had a second chance to build their own country and their own form of government. Perhaps if the rebels had not made the attempt, our ancestors would not have felt obliged to try new ideas. Even failures can make a difference.

The Red River Rebellion

When the Fathers of Confederation chose a motto for Canada, they found it in the Bible: "For He shall have dominion also from sea unto sea." The Latin *A mare usque ad mare*, which forms the Canadian motto, means "from sea to sea."

Of course the new Dominion of Canada formed by Confederation in 1867 did not stretch from sea to sea. It was made up of only Nova Scotia, New Brunswick and the southern parts of present-day Quebec and Ontario. However, the founders of Canada had had a dream. Someday, their country would stretch all the way to the Pacific Ocean. A few million Canadians would extend their influence across the huge, empty prairies, through the Rocky Mountains to the scattered settlements of British Columbia.

The odds against success were great. The distances were vast and the costs enormous. Already the Americans wanted the Northwest with its rich resources and unlimited space for expansion. But what both the Americans and the Canadians forgot was that the people of the Northwest had their own ideas about the future. They had learned to live on the prairies and had developed their own ways. Their desire was to live undisturbed. Their dream and the Canadian dream could not exist simultaneously.

Since 1670, authority over what is now western and northern Canada had rested with the Hudson's Bay Company. Left to itself, the company simply did what it wanted—traded furs and made money. It wasted little on guns and soldiers. It had no schemes to convert Indians to Christianity or to bring out

51

settlers. Both would have hurt the fur trade by altering the native way of life.

Instead, the fur trade created its own society. English-speaking traders and French-speaking *voyageurs* took Indian wives, and their offspring called themselves *Métis*. While some settled down to farming or trading, most Métis loved their freedom. Once a year, for the great buffalo hunt, they accepted discipline. More than a thousand Métis men, women and children set off each summer to track buffalo across the land of the fierce Sioux. In 1851, fewer than a hundred Métis fought off twenty times their number of Sioux in a two-day battle at Grand Coteau. It was the proudest memory of a people who called themselves the "New Nation."

In 1812, the Hudson's Bay Company allowed Lord Selkirk to bring Scottish immigrants to settle among the Métis who made their homes along the Red River. The early years brought floods, crop failure and starvation to the Selkirk settlers but they survived. Former Swiss and British soldiers also settled in the colony. By 1867, the Red River colony had about ten thousand people. Most were Métis, the rest were Catholic missionaries, Selkirk settlers, traders and Hudson's Bay officials. For all the differences among its inhabitants, the colony was peaceful. The Hudson's Bay Company appointed a governor and a governing council. Although this system was undemocratic, it had the support of the Red River community.

People at Red River might have been content, but Britain worried about how long such a government could last against American pressure to expand northward. In 1846, the Hudson's Bay Company had lost control of the rich Oregon Territory when American settlers poured over the mountains. Would the Red River be next? In 1857, the British Parliament decided the best answer would be to hand the whole territory over to Canada.

The idea was appealing to the Canadians. Two explorers, Henry Hind and Simon Dawson, sent back glowing reports of the Territories' rich potential . Soon, a trickle of Ontario farmers headed west to find new land. Other Canadians, such as young Dr. John Schultz, joined free traders in the new village of

Winnipeg a little south of the Hudson's Bay headquarters at Fort
Garry. There Dr. Schultz opened a store. The Canadians were
not popular in their adopted settlements. They disapproved of
mixed marriages and called the easygoing Métis lazy. Dr. Schultz
bought the only newspaper in the colony and used it to attack the
Hudson's Bay Company. Older settlers resented being told what
to do by pushy newcomers. Meanwhile the Americans were
trying to make inroads into the Northwest. They made a special
effort to win friends among the Métis. A French-speaking American consul, Oscar Malmros, opened an office in Winnipeg. An
Irish-American, W.B. O'Donoghue, became a teacher at the new
Catholic school across the Red River at St. Boniface.

In Ottawa, Canada's new prime minister, Sir John A.
Macdonald, would soon learn the problems of trying to build a
nation from sea to sea. From John Schultz in Winnipeg came
warnings of Yankee conspirators. Across the river, Bishop
Alexandre Taché sent a warning to Macdonald's Quebec ally,
George - Etienne Cartier: the Red River people, especially the
Métis, were not eager to be absorbed into Canada. Macdonald
was more worried by the Americans than by the Métis. His
enemy, George Brown of the Toronto *Globe*, demanded immedi-
ate action to stop American expansion. So did a band of young
men who called their group "Canada First." Cartier, always an
optimist, believed that Métis fears could easily be calmed.
William McDougall, a former ally of Brown who had switched his
support to Macdonald, added his influence. For years, Mc-
Dougall had argued for expansion to the Northwest. Now was his
chance. In the spring of 1868, Cartier and McDougall set off for
London, England, to arrange for the transfer of land from the
Hudson's Bay Company to Canada. It was all amazingly easy. In
exchange for some land and a cash payment of $1.5 million, the
entire territory of the Hudson's Bay Company would be transferred to Canada on December 1, 1869.

In Ottawa, even penny-pinching critics admitted that Canada had gotten a bargain. All other problems, Macdonald believed, would solve themselves. The Hudson's Bay Company
could still trade furs. Treaties would settle Indian land claims. At

the Red River settlement, nothing would change. Ottawa would appoint a governor and fifteen councillors. Part of their job would be to find out what kind of local government the people really wanted.

Unfortunately for Canada, it was not that simple. At the Red River, everybody had a grievance. Hudson's Bay officials wanted their share of the Canadian cash payment. Other settlers grumbled about not having been consulted. None worried more than the Métis, who feared that their entire way of life as hunters and boatmen would vanish. As if to warn of approaching tragedy, drought and grasshoppers wiped out the Red River's crops in the summer of 1868 and hunting parties failed to find buffalo. The colony faced starvation.

Ottawa tried to help. A Canadian road crew arrived with orders to begin work on a route from the Red River to Lake Superior. Surely that would bring jobs and money to the desperate colony. The idea backfired. Catholic missionaries noted that no French Canadians had come with the party. Few local people got jobs and they were paid only with credit at Dr. Schultz's store. The move added to suspicions that the Red River would soon be overrun by still more greedy, overbearing Canadians.

Then Ottawa made another mistake. No one had a longer record of urging Canada's westward expansion than William McDougall. Frankly, no one could be more easily spared from Ottawa than the vain, tiresome politician known as "Wandering Willy." In the summer of 1869, the government announced that McDougall would be Canada's first governor of the Red River. The choice was not welcomed. People in the Red River suspected that McDougall's only supporters were land-hungry, Protestant farmers from Ontario. He would bring these supporters swarming in like bees, they said.

Canadian land surveyors reached the colony in August. Their leader, Colonel J. Stoughton Dennis, agreed to start work as far from the Métis land holdings as possible, but the party's purpose was clear. Before the Ontario farmers could occupy the land, it must be neatly divided. The colony's leaders could have reassured the people but they preferred not to. Governor William closed his *Colonial Advocate*. He had been too busy with politics and too saddened by the death of his youngest son to carry on. In the summer of 1836, after his defeat, Mackenzie started a new paper, the *Constitution*, in which he continued to try to persuade Upper Canadians to overthrow the yoke of British domination.

As the months passed, the more patient Reformers began to see that their time would come again. The new "bread and butter" legislature happily ordered new roads, harbors, and canals and borrowed $4 million to pay for them, but suddenly the terrible economic slump of 1837 swept across the United States and hit Upper Canada. In a few weeks, confidence vanished. People raced to the banks to withdraw their money only to find the doors locked. Bankers demanded that loans be paid back and hundreds of businessmen and farmers faced ruin. In Montreal, bankers were helped by the colonial government. In Toronto, even the Family Compact was furious when Sir Francis did nothing to help them. Across the province people who had cheered the lieutenant governor a year before now cursed him for their troubles.

To Mackenzie, the terrible economic crisis of 1837 was too good a chance to miss. Why wait for the next election? In his old political stronghold "back of the ridges", north of Toronto, there were hundreds, perhaps thousands of people eager to overthrow the inefficient government. Samuel Lount, a blacksmith from Holland Landing who had sat with Mackenzie in the Assembly, joined him now. So did others. Through the spring and early summer, Mackenzie travelled through the familiar country, urging, persuading and arousing his old supporters.

To his credit, Mackenzie knew he was not a popular leader. One of the respected, trusted Reform leaders must take charge. Bidwell refused; so did Robert Baldwin. Only a nervous John Rolph attended the hushed, fervent meeting at Doel's Brewery in Toronto, where a declaration was passed that only just fell short of proclaiming Upper Canada independent. A Committee of Vigilance was formed.

Again Mackenzie headed north, gathering a bodyguard of young horsemen to protect him from hostile Tory farmers. By

This picture of Louis Riel was taken around 1878, a few years after the collapse of his provisional government at Red River.

Mactavish, dying of tuberculosis at Fort Garry, lacked the will and the energy. Bishop Taché had left for Rome.

The Métis Organize

In fact, only one group in the whole colony was organized to speak for themselves. It was the traditional Métis who could turn to the military system of the hunt as a way of organizing resistance. Fuelled by the threat of extinction of their way of life, they chose a leader they felt could stand up to the Canadians on his own terms—Louis Riel.

Riel's Métis father had given him a burning pride in the Métis as a nation. His mother, daughter of the first white woman in the West, had made him a devout Catholic. In 1858 Bishop Taché had chosen young Louis, then fourteen, to be educated in Montreal, hoping he would become the first Métis priest. Louis was a quick student, but he was painfully homesick. In 1865, he abandoned school, spent a few unhappy years in Montreal and by the summer of 1868, drifted back to the Red River.

Riel was like many of the young men who had flocked to Papineau before 1837. His education made him unfit for frontier life, but had given him a store of ideas looking for an opportunity. He turned to politics as an outlet for his intellectual energies and his hostility against the Canadians. A politician needs an audience and Riel found his easily among the Métis. His subject was always the same: the Canadian surveyors were plotting to take Métis land. On October 11, 1869, when a survey party reached André Nault's farm, eighteen Métis, led by Riel, drove them away. Suddenly Riel was a hero. When Métis leaders met at St. Norbert to discuss their future, the older men were ignored. The young buffalo hunters and the fur trappers were back from the plains and they wanted action. Riel was their man.

The St. Norbert Métis formed a "National Committee." Riel was its secretary. On October 21, a party of armed Métis rode south, put up a barrier at the Pembina border crossing and left a blunt message for the approaching Canadian governor: "The National Committee of the Métis of Red River orders William McDougall not to enter the Territory of the Northwest without special permission of the above-mentioned committee."

No self-appointed committee could give such an order to government officials and Riel knew it. How would the government of the colony respond? On October 25, the Company-appointed Council of Assiniboia summoned the leading Métis, scolded them and waited for Riel's explanation. The Métis, Riel said, were "uneducated and only half-civilized." If McDougall was not forced to respect their rights, new settlers would soon crowd them out. Nervously, the council debated what to do next. Two Métis members of the council agreed to ride to Pembina to persuade Riel's followers to take down the barricade. They were unsuccessful.

When McDougall reached Pembina on October 30, he dismissed the order of the National Committee as "contemptuous and insulting." However, neither he nor his two companions got past the Métis guards. "A King without a Kingdom is said to be poorer than a peasant," sneered an American reporter, "and I can assure you that a live Governor with a full complement of officials and menials... without one poor foot of territory, is a spectacle sad enough to move the hardest heart."

With four hundred armed Métis behind him, Riel was the only man with power in the colony. He proved it on November 2 by seizing Fort Garry. Now he controlled the biggest store of food, clothing and money in the Red River. Everyone waited to see what he would do next. Though few people understood it at the time, Louis Riel did not want to be a dictator. Nor, despite the encouragement of Malmros and O'Donoghue, did he want to hand the Red River over to the Americans. Instead, Riel wanted all the people of the colony — white and Métis — to give him power to negotiate with Canada. Since only the Hudson's Bay Company had legal authority, Riel had to destroy its power. Because Canada would respect him only if he showed that he was in complete control, he must persuade or even force the Red River people to obey him.

The Red River community was frightened and divided. English-speaking settlers and even many Métis feared the rough buffalo hunters and their excitable leader, and they wanted to avoid an armed conflict. When Riel invited all the people to send delegates to Fort Garry on November 16, they agreed with him that there should be a temporary or "provisional" government. What about McDougall? English-speaking delegates wanted to allow him to enter. The Métis insisted he stay out. Riel quickly found a compromise. As soon as the would-be governor agreed to a list of rights, he could come to Fort Garry. The colony must have its own elected legislature. It must also send members to Parliament in Ottawa. All the old rights and customs of the Red River must be respected. Red River residents must be able to keep their land, even if they had no legal papers to prove they owned it.

One group had purposely not been invited to Fort Garry. Unpopular and out of touch, Schultz and his fellow Canadians had awakened slowly to the shocking threat Riel and the Métis posed to the early union with Canada. If the Hudson's Bay Company or the Selkirk settlers were too timid to act, it was up to the few Canadians to save the Red River from the Americans who would surely move in and take over if the Canadians did not get there first. Messengers galloped south to warn McDougall. On December 1, whatever happened, he must proclaim the Hudson's Bay territories to be part of Canada. That would be a signal for all loyal subjects to overthrow Riel.

McDougall Fights

An angry, humiliated McDougall needed no encouragement. Commonsense would have told him that the Canadians at the Red River were too weak to beat Riel. His orders from Ottawa told him to wait, but McDougall ignored them. On December 1, with an icy wind whipping his coattails, he stepped across the border, pulled a little Union Jack out of his pocket and read the proclamation which united Rupert's Land and the Northwest to Canada. Then he walked back to his hotel and wrote a letter to Colonel Dennis in Winnipeg: as "conservator of the peace," Dennis must attack Riel's provisional government.

When Dennis looked around at the excited but ill-armed Canadians at Schultz's store, he wisely refused the honor. When Riel heard of McDougall's proclamation, he was furious. Next day, Métis seized Schultz's newspaper and raided Winnipeg houses for rifles. After waiting a week for the Canadians to attack, Riel collected six hundred armed followers and a couple of cannons and marched out to Schultz's store. The Canadian leader and forty-five men gave up. Soon Schultz and his men were crowded into the unheated jail cells at Fort Garry.

Six days after his proclamation, McDougall opened his first mail from Ottawa. His heart sank. For the first time, he learned that Ottawa had cancelled the date of transfer. The Red River colony, warned Prime Minister Macdonald, was a foreign country. By his proclamation, McDougall had given the Hudson's Bay Company an excuse to give up its burden. Ottawa had done its best to stay clear of the new responsibility until it could take over peacefully. McDougall had ruined everything.

At Fort Garry, Riel was triumphant. The day after he captured Schultz, he issued a "Declaration of the People of Rupert's Land and the Northwest," explaining that the Red River people had a right to form their own government. Hadn't the Hudson's Bay Company abandoned them to Canadian tyranny? The Union Jack was taken down and a new flag was hoisted over Fort Garry—white with a gold *fleur de lys* and a green shamrock. To pay his men, Riel seized money and supplies from the Hudson's Bay Company stores.

Sir John A. Macdonald soon got over his anger. He knew that no wise politician holds a grudge for long and thought he could buy Riel off by giving the Métis leader a government position.

In December the government sent off fresh envoys, this time from Quebec. They were Father J.G. Thibault, Colonel Charles de Salaberry and Donald A. Smith. The most important of these was Smith. A tough, self-made man, Smith had moved from a lonely Labrador trading post to become the wealthy head of Hudson's Bay Company operations in Canada. Donald Smith had never set foot in the West before. However, if the company was to hand over its territory and collect its money, it was up to Smith to complete the deal.

It is hard to imagine a harder mission. The Canadian government gave Smith no special powers, neither did the Hudson's Bay Company. Even Father Thibault and Colonel de Salaberry worked against him. Yet, if Smith failed, both Canada's dream of a coast-to-coast nation and his own position in the Hudson's Bay Company would be lost. There was only one thing he could do. He must divide the people and cut away Riel's support.

The Bitterness Grows

Once admitted to the colony, Smith played his cards carefully. His instructions, he explained, had been left behind in the United States. He would read them only to the assembled people. Riel tried desperately to find out what they contained. Foiled, he agreed to summon a meeting on January 19, 1870. More than a thousand people crowded into Fort Garry, standing for hours in

On January 19, 1870, a large crowd assembled in Fort Garry
to hear the Canadian government's envoy, Donald Smith.
Riel translated for the French-speaking Métis.

the clear, bitterly cold weather as Smith spoke. Of course, Smith really had no instructions. He seized the chance to argue for union with Canada. An embarrassed Riel stood at his side, translating into French. By afternoon, the crowd was won over. There were cheers and shouts for the prisoners to be released. Smith had won.

Or had he? That night, Father Thibault, Colonel de Salaberry, and a local priest worked furiously to revive suspicions. How could the Métis trust an Englishman like Smith? What guarantees had he brought? Next day, the crowd gathered again. Riel spoke carefully and persuasively. Why not choose twenty delegates from each of the French and English communities? Let them decide what was best. Now it was Riel's turn to be cheered.

"We are not yet enemies," Riel told the people, "but we came very near being so."

Never before had the Red River people had an election. There was much excitement as delegates were picked. With argument and a few small bribes, Donald Smith persuaded the Métis parishes to elect three of Riel's opponents, including Riel's cousin, Charles Nolin. At Winnipeg, the American group triumphed, choosing a bartender named Alfred Scott. On January 26, the convention met and soon a six-man committee was busy listing demands. Everything went well until the committee reported. Riel spoke up. The colony, he insisted, must also become a full province of Canada. Most delegates disagreed. Twice they voted against Riel's idea. He was furious. "The devil take it, we must win!" he shouted. "The vote may go as it likes but the measure must be carried."

In his rage, Riel arrested Hudson's Bay officials and leading citizens. He even posted guards in Governor Mactavish's sickroom. It was Donald Smith who suggested a way out. Why not send representatives to Ottawa? Immediately Riel was pleased. That was what he had always wanted. Meanwhile, how would the colony be governed? The English-speaking delegates were worried. They did not trust Riel, but Governor Mactavish was too sick to take charge. They wanted to ask their people but Riel allowed no delay. On February 10, all but three of the forty delegates voted for a new provisional government. Riel would be president. William O'Donoghue, the American leader, would be treasurer. Tension broke in a burst of rejoicing. All the prisoners were released. Fireworks, stored in Schultz's warehouse, celebrated Riel's government, and "a regular drunk commenced in which every one seemed to join."

Not all the Canadians had waited for their freedom. Several had escaped. Thomas Scott, a bold young Ontarian, had broken out on January 9 and trudged through the snow to Portage la Prairie. Two weeks later Schultz had squeezed through a cell window. His makeshift rope snapped and he twisted his leg but somehow he got away to the Scottish settlements. Both men wanted revenge. Among young Canadians and a few of the white settlers, they found eager supporters. Others warned that it was crazy to attack Riel. His Métis were too strong. Major Charles Boulton, a member of the Canadian survey party and a former British army officer, pleaded with Scott to reconsider. When Scott insisted, Boulton agreed to be leader. Perhaps he could save the fiery young Canadians from disaster.

On February 12, a hundred young men set out. At Headingley, a raging blizzard held them for two days, but not even the news of the successful convention could stop them. After a futile raid on Winnipeg on the night of the 14th, they ran into Schultz north of Fort Garry at Kildonan, with his own following and a little brass cannon. So far, all had been marching and talk. Suddenly there was tragedy. A young Métis prisoner, Norbert Parisien, escaped, shooting Hugh Sutherland, the son of respected Scottish settlers. Under the tearful appeals of Mrs. Sutherland and the Kildonan women, Schultz's men retired. Boulton's men gave up their plans. However, in a last brave show, they decided to march home past Fort Garry.

Next morning, as Boulton's men straggled through deep snow past the fort, Métis horsemen galloped over the drifts and surrounded them. On Boulton's command, the Canadians surrendered. Soon all of them were in the ice-cold Fort Garry cells. Riel had planned to kill his old enemy, Dr. Schultz. Disappointed, he planned to execute Boulton instead. As the news spread, the colony was horrified. Even Oscar Malmros pleaded for Boulton. So did the grieving Sutherlands. It was Donald Smith who carried the issue. Killing Boulton, he explained, would split the colony forever. If Boulton were spared, Smith would promise to bring the English settlers into line. Exhausted and racked by his responsibility, Riel broke down and cried. Boulton would live. Indeed, he told the startled Canadian leader, he would make Boulton leader of the English.

Riel's strain was understandable. Everything depended on him, an inexperienced young Métis. Schultz was still free and probably plotting more trouble. Indian war parties were reportedly close by. Food and money were running out. Delegates to Ottawa must be chosen. His Métis soldiers wanted more pay.

They were angry that Boulton had escaped. Now they complained about their other prisoners—especially Tom Scott.

The Execution of Thomas Scott

To Riel, Scott was nothing but a troublemaker. He was rude to the guards, and he had tried to escape. On February 28, guards dragged Scott from his cell and would have beaten him to death if a Métis councillor had not stepped in. Scott was not grateful. He shouted insults at Riel when the Métis leader appeared. Immediately Scott was chained to a wall. On March 3, Riel ordered a court martial according to the simple rules of the buffalo hunt. Evidence was heard and then Scott was brought in. Riel was both witness and interpreter. The president of the court called for the verdict from the jury. Some wanted exile; most demanded death. The majority won.

Once again the colony was shocked by Riel's actions. This time not even Smith could influence Riel. "We must make Canada respect us," the Métis leader shouted. At noon on March 4, guards led Scott to a ditch outside the fort. Riel stood nervously on the edge of the crowd. Six Métis took up their rifles. Only five fired. Another Métis finished off the writhing Canadian with a single revolver shot.

Perhaps the Métis were satisfied with Scott's death. Certainly the Red River colony was frightened. However, Canada would never forgive Riel. Until March 4, Riel could possibly have had the political career he always sought. Now the ghost of Tom Scott made this ambition impossible.

Too late to save Scott, Bishop Taché came home to the Red River on March 8. In Ottawa, before the execution, he had found Canadian ministers "in the main" satisfied with the Red River demands. Riel was overjoyed at the news. In Bishop Taché's honor, all the remaining prisoners were released. Soon, the three delegates left on the long journey to Ottawa. One of them, Judge John Black, could speak for the Hudson's Bay Company and the English settlers. The others were Riel's men. Grim, dark-bearded Father Ritchot had been Riel's advisor from the start. Alfred Scott, the American bartender, would follow his lead.

Donald Smith had promised the delegates a cordial welcome but public feeling was strongly against them. Instead of hiding in the colony, Schultz and his Ontario friends summoned meetings. Crowds strained to see the bloodstained ropes that had supposedly tied Scott's hands. Liberal politicians turned public anger against their Conservative opponents in Ottawa. "Riel and his accomplices have taken the life of a Canadian," raged the Toronto *Globe*. Among the accomplices must be the delegates from the Red River. The Macdonald government did its best to protect its three guests. A policeman escorted them to Ottawa. When Scott's brother had two delegates arrested, government lawyers had them set free. Prime Minister Macdonald was caught between the English and the French. While Ontario wanted vengeance, Montreal newspapers accused the government of trying to start a Protestant colony in the West. In fact, as the delegates soon found out, all the prime minister wanted was a quick settlement before there was any more trouble.

Regardless of what the Red River people wanted, Riel had his wish. The little colony would immediately become a province. The rights of French and English, Catholic and Protestant, were guaranteed. The rights of minorities in language and education would be safe. All land ownership was confirmed and 1,400,000 acres of Red River land were set aside for the Métis. On May 12, the Manitoba Act passed its final hurdle in Ottawa. When the news reached the Red River, cannons at Fort Garry boomed out a twenty-one-gun salute.

Father Ritchot had one more duty. Ottawa must forgive all that had happened since the previous October. Louis Riel and his friends must receive full amnesty, or pardon, for their actions. Ottawa hesitated. Even now the Northwest was not part of Canada. Riel's rebellion had been against the Hudson's Bay Company. Perhaps the British government could help. Meanwhile, George - Etienne Cartier suggested, "Let Mr. Riel continue to maintain order and govern the country as he has done up to the present moment."

Ritchot was puzzled. Ottawa's apparent approval of Riel was in sharp contrast to preparations for a big military expedition to the Red River. Why should the British and Canadian governments send 2,000 soldiers to put down what people in the East called "Red River Rebellion"? The government wanted only a chance to show the flag and reassure the Indians, Cartier assured him. Half the Canadians would be enlisted in Quebec. Ritchot knew better. Colonel Garnet Wolseley, the British officer who commanded the expedition, wanted military glory. A third of his soldiers were tough British regulars. The young men in the Ontario battalion thirsted to avenge Scott.

By June 17, when Ritchot landed at Fort Garry, much had happened in the colony. Once again the Union Jack flew over the fort. O'Donoghue, who had tried to haul it down, was in disgrace. Most of Riel's Métis supporters had gone back to work for the Hudson's Bay Company. Only fifty armed men remained to defend his authority. Ritchot brought good news and bad. In Ottawa, every one of Riel's demands had been met. There was even a new lieutenant governor for the future province, a Nova Scotia lawyer named Adams G. Archibald. Quiet, bilingual, sensible, Archibald was everything McDougall was not. However, there was to be no amnesty for the rebels.

That summer, the only question in the colony was whether Governor Archibald or Wolseley's soldiers would arrive first. The soldiers had by far the harder journey. Canadian officials and contractors delayed preparations. At Sault Ste. Marie, Americans did their best to bar passage to the expedition. At Prince Arthur's Landing, Wolseley learned that a forest fire had destroyed most of the work on the trail.

By any standard, the Red River Expedition of 1870 was an amazing feat. In the heat of summer, under clouds of mosquitoes, Wolseley's men hauled boats, guns and supplies over forty-seven portages, through swamps and along streams so shallow the soldiers had to wade alongside. Much of the time it rained. Not a single man died and only a few fell sick. Wolseley gave credit to his own planning, good officers and his orders that the men drink nothing stronger than tea.

On the evening of August 23, in the pouring rain, Wolseley's men landed on the banks of the Red River a few miles north of

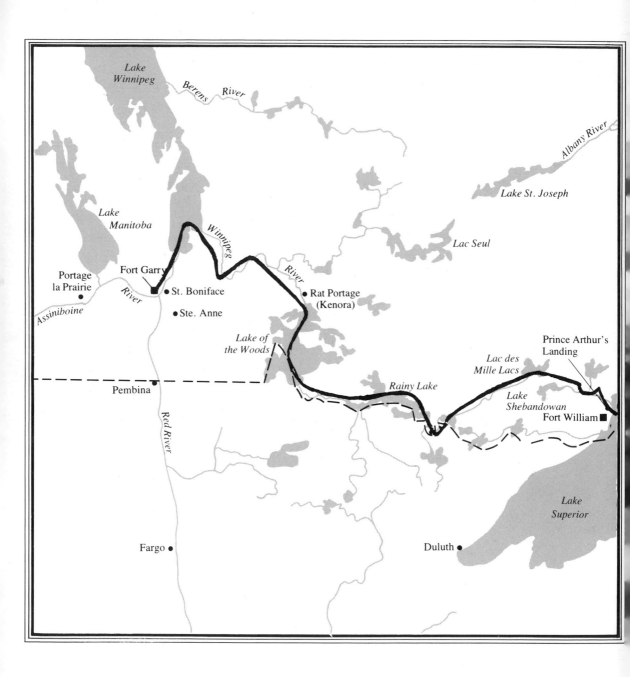

*Map showing the route taken
by Colonel Garnet Wolseley and
his troops in the summer of 1870.*

On August 23, 1870, 2,000 troops under Colonel Garnet Wolseley landed a few miles north of Fort Garry.

Fort Garry. From a hill just in sight of the campfires, a few men sat watching on horseback. Louis Riel wrestled with the same dilemma he had faced all summer. Should he fight? Should he flee? He rode back to Fort Garry. Next morning, the decision was made for him. A Hudson's Bay man flung open his door. "For the love of God clear out! The troops are only two miles from town."

Riel Flees

Riel fled. Far behind him, drenched and miserable, Wolseley's soldiers plodded through the mud. As the first men came around the walls, the gates of Fort Garry hung open. "Personally I was glad that Riel did not come out and surrender," Wolseley wrote, "...for then I could not have hanged him as I might have done had I taken him prisoner while in arms against his sovereign.'' So much for the errand of peace.

By the time Governor Archibald arrived, Wolseley and his British soldiers had left for eastern Canada. The Canadian militiamen soon established a sour reputation. Elzéar Goulet, one of Scott's firing squad, leaped into the Red River and drowned while trying to escape a mob of soldiers. André Nault, Riel's uncle, was beaten and left for dead on the prairie.

To Archibald fell the difficult task of ending the hatreds. ''You can hardly hope to carry on Responsible Government,'' he warned Ottawa, ''by inflicting death penalties on the majority of the electors.'' Manitoba's first government was a careful balance of English and French. The first premier, Henry Clarke, was a bilingual Catholic lawyer from Montreal. French-Canadian lawyers, brought to the Red River by Bishop Taché, filled key positions.

For Louis Riel there was no place in the politics of the province he had created and there was no pardon. He should go away for a few years, Taché urged, until all was forgotten. However, Riel could not face the homesickness, or swallow the bitterness of being denied his political career. Exhausted and frustrated, he became so sick that he almost died. Slowly, as 1871 slipped by, he regained his strength. Suddenly, both he and the Métis had a chance to prove their loyalty.

William O'Donoghue had fled the Red River for the United States. For months he pleaded with anyone who would listen that the former colony was ripe for American annexation. Only his fellow Irishmen of the radical Fenian Brotherhood, which fought for Irish independence from England, believed him. In 1866 and in 1870, the Fenians had tried to invade Canada. Now, in the fall of 1871, a few of them agreed to try again.

Governor Archibald had sent the troublesome militiamen home and Manitoba was defenceless. The governor exhorted the people of Manitoba to defend themselves. The Métis responded and Riel was listed as a lieutenant in one of the hurriedly organized military companies. The Fenian threat dissolved, but Archibald delightedly took the chance to thank Riel in person.

Sadly, that was not the end of troubles in the Northwest. In both Ontario and Quebec, the Red River Rebellion was too useful a political issue to forget. Ontario's new Liberal government put a price of $5,000 on Riel's head. In Catholic Quebec, politicians denounced Macdonald and Cartier for not defending the Métis leader. Through Bishop Taché, Macdonald offered Riel $1,000 to leave the country. Donald Smith added $3,000 of his own. Riel took the money but he could not bear to stay away. The Métis insisted on sending him to Parliament in 1873 and again in 1874. In 1874, braving the risk of arrest, Riel slipped into Ottawa, signed the House of Commons register and escaped. Later that year, the House voted to expel him.

His friend Ambroise Lépine was not so lucky. Arrested in 1873 and tried by a Manitoba jury, Lépine was convicted of the murder of Thomas Scott and sentenced to hang. It was 1870 all over again. Law and justice were forgotten as interests in Ontario and Quebec clashed. In Ottawa, a new Liberal government sat paralyzed by the crisis. The politicians were saved by the governor general, Lord Dufferin, who granted Lépine a reprieve. Dufferin's decision forced the government to take action. On February 12, 1875, Ottawa banished Riel and Lépine from Canada for five years.

Riel had made a single terrible mistake. If Thomas Scott had lived, Riel's own ambition could have been fulfilled. Up until that point, Riel had been successful. He had stopped the appointment of a conceited and thoughtless governor. He had defeated a faction of greedy, narrow-minded Canadians. He had brought French and English together at the Red River. He had forced Ottawa to treat the Red River as a province like Nova Scotia or Quebec, not as a powerless colony. Because of Thomas Scott's death, Riel became an outcast. The needless killing of a man was too dreadful a memory to be easily forgotten. It was a lesson others should have remembered fifteen years later.

The Northwest Rebellion: The Second Riel Rebellion

Deafness is not the only reason we do not hear. Sometimes we are so busy talking that we cannot hear. Sometimes we do not listen because we think we will not understand what is being said anyway.

In 1870, politicians in Ottawa were so busy with plans to build Canada that the few thousand people at the Red River colony were not heard. Fifteen years later, the government was listening but it was too late to satisfy angry Métis, Indians, and whites, who once again turned to Louis Riel as their leader and savior.

Settling the West was Canada's greatest achievement. In a few years, a quarter of a continent was occupied, linked with railways and turned into one of the most abundant food-producing regions of the world. All this was done under the shadow of the United States, and by a few million people who often showed little faith in themselves or in their leaders. Development was cautious and tight-fisted. Canada had no money to spare.

The Changing Times

One of Canada's achievements was that, by and large, the West was settled peacefully, without the frontier lawlessness and violence of the United States. This was partly due to the efficiency of the North West Mounted Police and partly to the role played by the Métis in smoothing relations between whites and Indians, as they had in the days of the fur trade. Another reason for a more peaceful Canadian West was that white settlement did not start until a terrible disaster had already greatly destroyed the Indian way of life.

That disaster was the disappearance of the buffalo. The signs had been coming for a long time. Guns and horses made it too easy to kill the buffalo. Whites, Indians and Métis slaughtered them for their coats and for their tongues, which were a great delicacy. In 1877, the government in the Northwest Territories ordered the hunt to stop. Indians and Métis protested. The ban was lifted. Two years later, the buffalo were gone. The buffalo hunt had strongly influenced life in western Canada. A man proved his courage in the hunt. Discontented Métis had moved west from Manitoba to be closer to the hunt. Indians depended on buffalo for food, clothing and shelter. The Métis, at least, did have other means of support. They could grow a little wheat or potatoes on their long, narrow plots. They could work as wagon drivers. The Indians knew no other way of life. The proud Blackfoot rode south because of a faint rumor of buffalo herds. They walked back, starving and hopeless.

The North West Mounted Police and government officials did what they could. At many posts, policemen gave up their own food to keep Indians from starving. But the proud people of the plains could not live forever on biscuits and bacon provided by the government. What was the best solution? Both missionaries and officials agreed. The Indians must become farmers. They must give up the freedom to roam. They must move to small reserves. The government would give them seeds, cattle, tools and advice.

Perhaps there was no choice. However, the experts forgot how hard it was to farm on the prairies. The growing season was short. After 1881, little rain fell. In 1883, almost all the crops in the West suffered frost damage. The Indians had no knowledge of farming and lacked the patience to sow their seeds, tend them and wait for harvest. In the meantime, they feared they would starve to death.

White officials also expected fast results. They hoped to convert the Indians from their centuries-old practices in a few years. In 1883, orders came from Ottawa. Cutbacks were needed, as the taxpayers refused to support welfare for Indians. By cutting off food, the government hoped that the Indians would be forced to settle down to farming, but these harsh orders did not change the Indians. The Mounted Police, forced to carry out the new orders, no longer had the Indians' confidence. At Battleford, in the summer of 1884, Indians attacked a government food store, and for the first time, the Mounted Police had to retreat.

If Indians were angry by 1884, so were the Métis. Some of them had lived in the Northwest since long before 1870. Others had come from Manitoba, full of bitterness at the influx of white settlers there and anxious to regain their old freedom. All of them wanted one thing: the same generous land settlement given to the Manitoba Métis in 1870. Dozens of petitions repeated the demand while Ottawa hesitated. Of course, the people who settled the Northwest before 1870 were entitled to land. How about the Métis who had sold their Manitoba grant? In St. Boniface, Archbishop Taché recommended that the Métis be given reserves like those given to the Indians, but the Métis rejected this solution, as they did not want to be dependent on the government. They were firm about retaining their dignity and freedom.

Meanwhile, white settlers took up more and more land. Like most pioneers, the newcomers were ambitious and discontented. Like the people of Upper Canada, they too wanted help from the government. They complained that the promises that had drawn them west, including the guarantee of prosperity, were not being fulfilled. Many had bought land near Prince Albert because they hoped that the railway would pass that way and that once the line was finished, their land would be much more valuable. Instead, the Canadian Pacific took a southern route through Regina and Calgary.

The angry farmers organized, wrote out a "Bill of Rights" and demanded a stronger voice in government. Frank Oliver, a frontier newspaper editor as outspoken as William Lyon Mackenzie, warned, "If history is to be taken as a guide, what would be plainer than that without rebellion, the people of the North-

*Gabriel Dumont commanded the Métis forces during
the Northwest Rebellion of 1885.*

west need expect nothing.'' Most of the unhappiness in the
Northwest came together in the District of Lorne. It included
new Métis settlements like Batoche, Indian reserves and the
white homesteads around Prince Albert. Lorne was the first

district in the Northwest to have the thousand people needed to elect a member to the Northwest Territorial Council. The people of Lorne — including the Métis — had elected a moderate. An angry minority of whites met in farmhouses and schoolhouses to spin more radical schemes. One of them, William Henry Jackson, an excitable young Ontarian, urged the homesteaders to work with their Métis neighbors, and eventually Métis leaders like Gabriel Dumont and Charles Nolin began to attend these meetings.

Always the discussions led back to one problem. Who would take their complaints to the government? People kept coming up with the same answer. Fifteen years before, Riel had forced Ottawa to listen to their complaints. He could do it again. On May 6, 1884, the decision was made. A few days later, Dumont and three other Métis rode south with an invitation to Riel to come back to the Northwest and lead them.

Riel Returns

The years since 1870 had been terribly hard on Riel. Even in his youth, his friends had feared his wild rages and black moods. Being denied the one career he wanted, politics, had driven him mad. He had spent 1876 to 1878 in Quebec insane asylums. He came out, in the words of his doctor, "more or less cured." His life in ruins, Riel wandered back to the West and travelled with Indians and Métis as a trader. He became an American citizen in 1883 and settled down to the ill-paid, dreary life of a teacher at a small Catholic mission station in Montana.

Through the long, dismal years, one feeling kept Riel going: his deep sense of having been chosen to perform an important mission. In 1874, a letter from Bishop Ignace Bourget of Montreal to Riel gave voice to this feeling: "God, who has always led you and assisted you up to the present time, will not abandon you in the darkest hour of your life. For he has given you a mission which you must fulfil in all respects." Tied to Riel's sense of mission was a sense of personal grievance. Riel had given the Red River colony to Canada and never had his debt been repaid. Surely Ottawa owed him a rich reward for his services, he reasoned. Instead, he had wandered as a penniless fugitive. He was unable to support his aging mother, his wife and two children. When Dumont and his friends found Riel at the Montana mission, they needed little argument to persuade Riel to join them. From the people of Lorne had come a summons that could regain his political career for him.

News that Riel had arrived travelled fast. On July 19, a packed audience in Prince Albert heard him speak for the first time. If anything, his dignified, calm tone was not radical enough for them. The Catholic missionaries felt differently, however. They soon realized that Riel was unbalanced and that he saw himself as having been chosen by God as the savior of the Métis, many of whom believed him. On September 24, prominent Catholic clergy helped Riel found the Union of St. Joseph as a national Métis society. Instead of reinforcing their authority over Riel's supporters, however, they succeeded only in increasing his importance. The Church was not the only group that came to regret having enlisted Riel. Early white settler support dried up when word came that Riel had met with rebellious Indian leaders like Big Bear. For the whites and even most Métis, no anger at Ottawa could justify risking an Indian war.

Riel's official reason for being in the Northwest was to list the grievances of its people. By mid-December, he was finished. The list was long, ranging from Métis land claims to a demand by white settlers for a railway to Hudson Bay. Riel's own claims filled a prominent place. Like previous documents, the petition went to Ottawa, was politely received, and apparently ignored.

Riel's presence continued to divide the whites and Métis and upset the clergy. Father Alexis André, a missionary to the Métis, reported that Riel's demands ranged from $35,000 to $100,000. "My name is Riel and I want material," the Métis leader joked. At Regina, Edgar Dewdney, lieutenant governor of the Northwest Territories, offered to negotiate with Riel, but Ottawa was silent.

Perhaps it would have been better if Riel had chosen to return to the United States. Since the previous summer, he had lived on the charity of his people, which humiliated him. Yet he had rediscovered the joy of power. A solid core of Métis found his faith more convincing than the religion of their priests. His claims that Rome had fallen, that a new church must come to Canada with Bishop Bourget as its pope, made Riel's followers think that he heard the voice of God. When, on February 24, he announced that he must leave, an emotional crowd insisted he stay. Riel had staged the meeting, of course, to arouse such an appeal, but nevertheless he interpreted the results as God's will.

Fifteen years earlier, the Dominion of Canada had been forced to listen to a young man of barely twenty-six years. Once again, as leader of his people, Riel would force Ottawa to listen and he would do it the same way, by creating a provisional government. He would unite the Métis and the Indians. The messages from his night-long prayers told Riel that God was with him. The missionaries pleaded for delay. Riel agreed to a week of prayer and sent more messengers south and west, calling for support. On March 18, one of them returned. North West Mounted Police Commissioner Acheson Gosford Irvine was coming from Regina with hundreds of police. The Métis would all be arrested.

At once, Riel summoned his supporters. Armed Métis seized government officials. Next day was the feast of St. Joseph. Outside the church at Batoche, Riel announced his council. The Métis marvelled at its title — "Exovedate" — a word Riel had invented to mean "taken from the flock." A white flag bearing the Ten Commandments fluttered up a pole to become the new government's standard.

In 1869, the Hudson's Bay Company had had no one who dared face the tough Métis buffalo hunters. In 1885, the Canadian government had the North West Mounted Police. At Fort Carlton, Superintendent Garnet Crozier had collected sixty policemen and fifty special constables from Prince Albert. On March 21, an odd message reached the hot-tempered Irish police officer. Crozier and his men must surrender at once to Riel or be wiped out. Crozier was not impressed. Instead, on March 26, he ordered a few men to collect supplies from a little store near Duck Lake, halfway to Batoche. Under Gabriel Dumont, Métis met the policemen and ordered them back to Fort Carlton. Crozier and his men were outraged. Though Commissioner Irvine was due any moment with about a hundred more men, Crozier would not wait. With a hundred police and specials riding on sleighs, he set out down the snowy trail to Duck Lake.

The Fighting Begins

When the police arrived, Riel and three hundred Métis and Indians had joined Dumont. Crozier walked forward to negotiate. There were words. Shots rang out and an Indian and Dumont's brother fell dead. Riel's men, hidden in the woods on both sides of the trail, poured rifle fire down on the police and volunteers. In minutes, twelve of them lay dead or dying. Crozier and many others were hit. Amid terrified horses, Crozier turned his column and the survivors fled for safety. A horrified Riel, armed only with a crucifix, commanded his men to stop shooting. The battle of Duck Lake was over. The second Riel Rebellion had begun.

Until the shooting, few had believed a real outbreak was possible. Not even Crozier's men expected to fight. As news of Duck Lake spread, so did panic. Settlers abandoned their homes and raced for safety. More than five hundred men, women and children jammed the tiny police fort at Battleford. Prairie settlements from the Rockies to Winnipeg pleaded for guns and soldiers.

In turn, the settlers' terror excited the Indians. Near Battleford, young men from Poundmaker's reserve galloped into town to pillage the abandoned houses. At Eagle Hills, Indians killed their farm instructor. On April 2, Indians of Big Bear's band killed nine whites, including two priests. Two women and another man became prisoners. At nearby Fort Pitt, the tiny police garrison escaped downriver on a leaky barge.

Within hours of Crozier's disaster, Irvine reached Fort Carlton. That night, a fire broke out in the old wooden buildings. Police and volunteers collected the wounded, buried supplies under the ice and set out for Prince Albert. From Frog Lake to Carlton, the whole of North Saskatchewan was abandoned to Louis Riel. Riel's supporters were ecstatic. Victory proved that

*Eastern troops travelling to the Northwest in
1885 by the new Canadian Pacific Railway.*

God favored their leader. In their joy, they forgot that much of
Riel's plan had not worked. The Métis had failed to capture
Crozier and his men. Soon more soldiers and police would come
and Riel's men lacked good rifles and ammunition. Messengers to
the English-speaking Métis returned with gloomy news. Many of
them supported the government.

Even the French-speaking Métis were badly divided. Older
Métis resented the angry newcomers from the Red River. They
feared the government's vengeance. They were shocked by
Riel's rages and his attacks on the Catholic missionaries. Once
again, Charles Nolin had turned against Riel. Threatened with
death, Nolin fled to Prince Albert. Vengeance was coming. A
month before, Sir John A. Macdonald had announced the establishment of a commission with power to give land to the original
Métis settlers. There would be nothing for the people from the

Red River and there would be nothing for Riel. There would be no bribe to persuade Riel to go back to Montana.

The old prime minister had a much bigger problem on his mind than the Métis. By the winter of 1885, his dream of a railway to the Pacific was in hopeless trouble. Huge construction costs in the Rocky Mountains and in the treacherous muskeg north of Lake Superior had swallowed millions. Parliament blocked further financing. If the line collapsed, the Bank of Montreal, some of Canada's richest men and Macdonald's Conservative party would be ruined.

Suddenly, news came of Duck Lake. In hours, the railway's manager, William Van Horne, announced that troops could travel west over the unfinished line. Men of Canada's tiny permanent army soon loaded their guns on railway flatcars to begin the journey. Armories in Toronto, Montreal and a dozen smaller towns filled with excited young militia volunteers. A legend was born that the CPR saved Canada in 1885. Indeed it was Louis Riel who saved the CPR.

A week before Crozier's defeat, Macdonald had sent the commander of Canada's militia to Winnipeg. Major-General Fred Middleton was a short, red-faced British veteran, sixty years of age. He was also an energetic, modern-minded soldier who mixed pomposity with great commonsense. In a West of panic-stricken Canadians, Middleton alone grasped the problem. The only way to protect the scattered settlements was to attack Riel at once. With each day, rebel support and the risk to the settlers would grow.

Yet everything stood in the way of speed. Most of the militiamen in the West had never even fired a shot. Horses would have to haul Middleton's guns and supplies, but there was no grass on the frozen prairie to feed them. Hundreds more wagons must be collected simply to carry hay. Middleton was not deterred. His soldiers would learn on the march. The Hudson's Bay Company must manage the supplies. On April 6, a bare ten days after Duck Lake, Middleton marched north from the CPR line. The rest of his men would have to catch up.

Those men survived a terrible ordeal. Not even Van Horne

General Middleton, commander of the government troops.

knew what it was like north of Lake Superior in April. Young
Canadians, most of them fresh from offices and factories, en-
dured freezing rain, snow blindness, bad food, and exhaustion.
More than three thousand of them survived the eight-day trek
from Dog Lake to Red Rock over the broken line. No one dared
admit that they could have travelled more cheaply, quickly, and
with American blessing, through the United States. It was more
important to the government to serve the interest of the CPR.

Orders met the soldiers as they reached Winnipeg. Some
would join Middleton at Clark's Crossing. Others, under Colonel
William Otter, went to Swift Current. They would board
steamers and travel downriver to provide Middleton with a small
army on the far side of the South Saskatchewan. Two forces
were needed to surround Batoche. French-Canadian soldiers
went west to Calgary. A retired British soldier, Major-General
Thomas Bland Strange, would lead them to fight Big Bear's
Indians. Perhaps it was wiser that they should not have to fight
the Métis.

The plan made sense. If the head of the rebellion was cut off,

SASKATCHEWAN

Saskatchewan Wood Crees *Frog Lake* *General Middleton*

Fort Saskatchewan

North **ALBERTA** Frenchman's Butte Prince Albert *River* *Duck Lake* *Saskatchewan River*

Fort Pitt Beardy Batoche
Poundmaker **Fort Carlton**

Battle River Cut Knife Hill Battleford *Fish Creek* Humboldt
Grizzly Bear and Lean Man Clarke's Crossing

Eagle Hills

Red Saskatoon
Deer *General Strange* *Bear Hills*

Lt. Col. Otter *General Middleton*

ASSINIBOIA

Calgary *South* *Saskatchewan River* *Qu'Appelle*

Red Deer River *Canadian* *Railway* Qu'Appelle
Regina

Bow River *Pacific* Swift Current

Blackfoot

*The government troops advanced against
the rebels in three columns, led by
Generals Middleton and Strange and
Colonel Otter. The main battles
were fought at Duck Lake, Cut Knife
Hill, Fish Creek, Batoche and
Frenchmen's Butte.*

The battle at Fish Creek had cost the Canadians forty dead and wounded and there were a dozen more places on the road to Batoche where Dumont might attack. Middleton was now at the limit of horse transport and supplies must come by steamer. The nearest ship, the S.S. *Northcote*, was hard aground. Exhausted, Middleton came close to despair.

On the day of the fight at Fish Creek, Colonel Otter's men reached Battleford. The besieged settlers—who far outnumbered the Indians—were safe. Now they must have revenge. On May 1, Otter led militia, police and armed settlers to attack the Indian camp. Instead, at Cut Knife Hill, it was the Indians who attacked the Canadians in a desperate fight to save their village. By noon on May 2, Otter and his men were in full retreat. The third battle of the campaign was a third defeat for the government's men.

A hundred miles away at Fish Creek, Canadian spirits slowly revived. On May 5, the *Northcote* finally appeared and unloaded men, supplies and firearms. Now Middleton had a new plan. He would march inland to avoid any more ambushes and attack Batoche from the rear. Meanwhile, the *Northcote*, with a guard of soldiers, would attack from the river. On May 7, the march resumed.

Dumont's men were not idle. While Riel prayed and recorded his dreams in a diary, the Métis dug trenches and hoisted a heavy ferry cable out of the river. Their plan was to catch the *Northcote* and roll it over like a toy boat on a rushing brook. Women and children fled into the woods along the river's edge to escape the shooting.

At 8 a.m. on May 9, the steamer appeared. Métis and soldiers blazed away at each other. The ferry cable snatched at the mast and funnels and tore them off. The *Northcote* slipped through. Its captain and engineer were Americans. Beyond Batoche, they refused to go back. They felt they had risked enough. Meanwhile, Middleton's men arrived unnoticed until their guns opened fire.

In minutes, the Métis swarmed up the banks and through the familiar woods. It was Fish Creek over again, with Canadians outlined at the top of the hill to Métis sharpshooters hidden in the

Government soldiers preparing for battle.

bush below. Once again, Middleton found his men nervous and shaken. Should he retreat? That could only cause panic. Instead, he ordered his wagons to come up and form a corral in the rear. It was there that the Canadians dug in to spend the night.

Few of them slept that night but there was no attack. Next morning, when they found themselves still alive, the Canadians' courage revived. Middleton cautiously sent them out to their old positions and they returned in high spirits. On May 11, the general tried a new approach. Leading his mounted scouts, he rode out to the east side of the Métis settlement. Dumont had dug trenches there as well, but to defend them Métis and Indians had to come racing from the south. Now Middleton saw what he must do.

Next day, May 12, Middleton again rode out with his scouts, this time bringing a cannon. When the gun fired, the rest of his men would know that Dumont's men had rushed to the east. As before, the Métis ran across to meet the apparent attack. Middleton ordered the gunners to fire. Back at the camp, nothing happened. Middleton rode back in a fury to be told that the cannon shot had not been heard.

That afternoon, the Canadian soldiers again marched out to their former positions south of Batoche. They were angry and impatient. On the left, a few soldiers appeared to be advancing northward toward Batoche. Suddenly, the whole line surged forward, shouting and cheering. Hundreds of Canadians raced down the hill. Middleton rushed from his tent, mounted his horse and galloped out to take control.

Many of the Métis still waited for an attack from the east. Those few who faced the Canadian attack were old and short of ammunition. They fought like heroes. The mad rush resulted in the killing of four Canadians and the wounding of twenty-five. Dumont stayed to the end, fighting beside a man of ninety-three. "Several times I said to him, 'Father, we must retreat.' And the old fellow replied, 'Wait a minute, I want to kill another Englishman'." Dumont escaped but Middleton's men found twenty-one dead Métis.

The start of the battle at Batoche, May 12, 1885.

Riel escaped too. During the battle, he had wandered among his people, carrying only a crucifix. Near the end, he had tried to negotiate but Dumont would not hear of it. At the end, when Riel crossed the river to move his family to a safer place, the two men separated. They did not meet again. After trying to find his friend, Dumont headed south for the United States and safety.

For three days, Riel wandered alone in the woods. As he walked, a final vision came to him. Instead of escaping, he would demand a great state trial. All his grievances, all the sufferings of the Métis, would finally be presented. On May 15, Riel surrendered to two Canadian scouts. Middleton reported: "I found him a mild-spoken and mild-looking man, with a short brown beard and an uneasy, frightened look about his eyes, which gradually disappeared as I talked with him." On orders from Ottawa, Middleton sent his prisoner to the police barracks at Regina.

From Batoche, the soldiers marched north to Prince Albert and then travelled by steamer to Battleford. Middleton was right. Without Riel, the rebellion was over. On May 27, General Strange's soldiers failed to drive Big Bear's band from a big hill called Frenchmen's Butte, but the Indians fled after their brief success. Although four columns of militia failed to catch him, Big Bear surrendered to a surprised police sergeant at Fort Carlton on July 2. The rebellion ended almost where it had begun. At last the soldiers could go home to receive their medals and collect their memories.

The Trial of Louis Riel

The rebellion was over but the tragedy was not complete. For his great state trial, Riel would face a mere police magistrate and a six-man jury. During the eight weeks before his trial, Riel sat at Commissioner Irvine's desk, writing poetry and religious meditations and trying to think of ways to support his penniless family. He pleaded with Dewdney that his trial be moved to Ottawa so that he would be able to blame his misfortunes on the Liberals who had once set a price on his head. The proposal only proved, his jailer noted, that poor Riel was "cracked."

The prime minister's plans were a little different. Ottawa

The trial of Louis Riel began on July 28, 1885, in Regina.

would gladly have punished some of the Prince Albert farmers who had stirred up sedition in 1884. Except for Jackson, now obviously insane, they had covered their tracks too well. The evidence of the Catholic priests and missionaries and the mounds of documents taken at Batoche allowed only one conclusion: without Riel, there could have been no rebellion.

Almost all of Canada agreed. Even Quebec had been horrified by the outbreak and by the slaughter of priests at Frog Lake. Quebec militia battalions had served in the campaign. Slowly, the feeling of horror faded. Sympathy welled up for Riel as a lonely French Canadian at the mercy of the English. The leader of Quebec's Liberals, Honoré Mercier, caught the new mood. His party sent its best lawyers to fight for Riel's life.

A sweltering makeshift courtroom in Regina saw the greatest legal drama in Canadian history. For a week, Riel's lawyers did all in their power to postpone the trial. Each time Judge Hugh Richardson thwarted them. When the trial began on July 28, only one way remained to save Riel: he must be proved insane.

Was Riel mad? What is insanity? These are questions that are not settled yet. In 1885, the answer was simpler. Was Riel so insane during the rebellion that he could not tell right from wrong? On that argument, Jackson had been sent to an insane asylum near Winnipeg. Could a man who heard voices and who claimed that Bishop Bourget was pope be sane? The lawyers from Quebec had a strong case. Their worst opponent was Riel himself, who furiously rejected the idea that he was mad. To call him insane made a mockery of all Riel had done. It made fools of the Métis for choosing a lunatic as leader. Again and again Riel demanded to be heard. His lawyers did all that they could to keep him silent. The judge was torn. Should Riel be muzzled and not be allowed to speak? Could he be allowed to overrule his own lawyers? Finally Judge Richardson decided. Riel could speak.

For an hour, Riel's words poured out. Sometimes he insisted on his sanity; sometimes he pleaded the Métis cause. Riel spoke in English, often struggling for the right word. At first, the room was tense with excitement. Later, in the stifling heat, eyelids drooped, attention wandered. "Are you done?" Richardson asked. Riel was finished. Next day, August 1, at 2:15 p.m., the small jury withdrew. An hour later, the members filed back. The verdict was guilty. The foreman, Francis Cosgrove, caught the judge's eye: "Your honor, I have been asked by my brother jurors to recommend the prisoner to the mercy of the Crown."

Again Riel could speak. This time he spoke as he had rehearsed during the weeks at the police barracks. His argument was clear. The jury had saved him from the stigma of madness. The courtroom was silent, waiting out politely the condemned man's right to speak. Drained and exhausted, Riel stopped. Judge

*Sir John A. Macdonald was prime minister of Canada at the time
of both the Red River and the Northwest rebellions.*

Richardson spoke. There could be no excuse for what Riel had
done. There was no hope of mercy. On September 18, Riel would
be hanged.

The Final Days of Riel

Of course, that was not the end. Riel's lawyers appealed through
every stage, all the way to Queen Victoria. Again and again the
date for the execution was put off. The real appeal was not to law
but to politics. Thanks to Honoré Mercier, Riel became a symbol
to French Canadians. Why had Jackson been spared while Riel
must die? It was because one was English, the other French. Riel
was condemned so that Sir John A. Macdonald could win votes
in Ontario.

It did not matter then or now that this was nonsense. Long
before Quebec opinion shifted, Sir John A. Macdonald had made
up his mind. Riel's offence was not the murder of Thomas Scott.

It was the crime of starting a war of Indians and Métis. Riel must die as a warning to anyone else who might try to stir up trouble in the Canadian West.

At 8 a.m. on November 16, 1885, guards came for Riel. In his last days, the Métis leader had returned to his childhood faith. The missionaries who had fought his influence and demanded his punishment were with him at the end. They were reciting the Lord's Prayer when the trap opened and Riel fell.

In Quebec, the flags flew at half mast. Merchants draped their windows in black. "Riel our brother is dead," Mercier roared out at the fifty thousand Montrealers who met him on November 22, "victim of his devotion to the cause of the Métis of whom he was the leader, victim of fanaticism and treason." Mercier was joined by young Wilfrid Laurier, the future Canadian prime minister, who said, "If I had been on the banks of the Saskatchewan, I, too, would have shouldered my musket."

Even before he died, Riel knew he was a symbol. "Sir John Macdonald is now committing me to death for the same reason I committed Scott," he explained, "because it is necessary for this country's good." Others would suffer too. Eighteen Métis faced trial but only seven faced prison terms. Few at the time showed much concern for the fate of native people. Eleven Indians were condemned to die and eight were hanged. Big Bear and Poundmaker, old chiefs who had held back their young men, suffered two long years in prison.

In 1837 and again in 1870, rebellion won concessions. After 1885, there were no winners. The land claims of Métis were settled but they would have been resolved anyway. The government found new farm instructors for the Indians and squeezed the food rations even more tightly. The main result was more suffering. The whites of the Northwest soon won their voice in Parliament but it was a voice that ignored the Indians and Métis.

In 1884, Frank Oliver had claimed that rebellion brought results. To the followers of Louis Riel, the statement proved false.

Selected Biographies

DUMONT, Gabriel
Born in the Assiniboia territory in 1838, the son of Isidore Dumont and Louise Laframboise, both Métis, Dumont grew up without formal education but acquired a reputation as a shrewd buffalo hunter and a brave fighting man.

In 1884, Dumont was one of the delegates who persuaded Louis Riel to return to the Northwest Territories. Riel appointed him adjutant general in command of the Métis forces. Dumont led his Métis to meet the advancing Canadian militia at Fish Creek on April 23, 1885 and was responsible for the defence of Batoche on May 9–12, 1885. After the defeat at Batoche, he escaped to the United States and lived there for several years, appearing in "Buffalo Bill's Wild West Show." He returned to Canada after being granted amnesty and lived undisturbed until his death on May 19, 1906.

DURHAM, John George Lambton, 1st earl of
Durham was born in England in 1792. In 1813, he was elected to the House of Commons where he was nicknamed "Radical Jack" because of his radical policies. In 1835, he was appointed British Ambassador to Russia. In 1837, at the time of the unrest in Upper and Lower Canada, he was appointed Governor-in-Chief of British North America with extraordinary powers as lord high commissioner.

On his arrival in Canada, Durham immediately dismissed the Executive Council and formed a new one. He then granted amnesty to all but a few leaders of the rebellion. Criticized for his actions by the British Government, Durham resigned towards the end of 1838. The report he prepared after his return to England advocated uniting Upper and Lower Canada and granting the colony responsible government. He died in England on July 28, 1840.

MACKENZIE, William Lyon
Born near Dundee, Scotland on March 12, 1795, the only son of Daniel and Elizabeth Mackenzie. He came to Canada in 1820 and went into business as a shopkeeper. In 1824, he founded the *Colonial Advocate* at Queenston, near Niagara Falls, then came to York (now Toronto) in November of that year. He soon became spokesman for the radical wing of the reform movement.

Elected to the Legislative Assembly of Upper Canada in 1828, Mackenzie played an active role from the outset. He was expelled in 1831 for his outspoken opposition to the government, re-elected five times and each time expelled. In 1834, he was elected the first mayor of the newly incorporated city of Toronto. He also regained his seat in the Assembly.

After the 1837 rebellion, which he inspired and led, he escaped to the United States, tried to launch a fresh rebellion and was finally imprisoned for breaking American neutrality laws. After a painful struggle to support his family by journalism, he returned to Canada under an amnesty in 1840. He entered the Legislative Assembly in 1851 but his influence was slight. He resigned his seat in 1858 and died in Toronto on August 28, 1861.

PAPINEAU, Louis-Joseph

Born in Montreal, October 7, 1786, son of Joseph Papineau and Rosalie Cherrier. He served as a militia officer in the War of 1812, was elected to the Legislative Assembly in 1814 and served as Speaker almost continuously from 1815 to 1837. As Speaker, he became known as the leader of the *patriotes*. Papineau's opposition policies led directly to the rebellion in 1837, but he tried, at the end, to stop the violence and fled to the United States soon after the outbreak.

Papineau lived in Paris from 1839 to 1845 when an amnesty allowed him to come home to Canada. He served in the Legislative Assembly of Canada from 1848 to 1851 and from 1852 to 1854, but to most members he was a figure from the past. He died on September 23, 1871.

RIEL, Louis "David"

Born at St. Boniface, Assiniboia on October 23, 1844, son of Louis Riel, a Métis, and Julie Lagimodière. In 1858, the young Riel was sent by Bishop Taché of St. Boniface to be educated at a seminary in Montreal.

When he returned to the Red River in 1868, his personal magnetism and worldly experience made him a natural spokesman for the Métis cause. In 1870 he became president of the provisional government organized by the Métis of the settlement. When it collapsed, Riel fled. The mental strain of the next few years was great, and Riel spent most of 1876 to 1878 in insane asylums in Quebec.

On his release he went west and settled in Montana. There he taught school, married Marguerite Belhumeur, a Métis, and became an American citizen.

In June, 1884, he was invited by a group of settlers, Métis and white, to return to Canada to lead a protest against the Canadian government's indifference to their grievances. When the ensuing rebellion collapsed, Riel surrendered to the Canadian forces. After his trial in July, he was sentenced to death and executed on November 16, 1885.

For Discussion

Why should we study our rebel ancestors? This was the question that began our study of rebellions in Canada. How would you answer the question?

LOWER CANADA

1) Who was Papineau?
2) Why was he discontented?
3) Why did many French Canadians agree with him?
4) Why did the rebellion fail?

UPPER CANADA

1) Who was Mackenzie?
2) Why was he discontented?
3) Why did many English Canadians agree with him?
4) Why did the rebellion fail?

RIEL REBELLIONS

1) Who was Riel?
2) Why was he discontented?
3) Why did many Métis agree with him?
4) Did both his rebellions fail? If so, why?
   If your answer is no, what reasons can you give for your opinion?

GENERAL

1) Put yourself into the rebellions.
   How would you have acted if you were the leader of a) French-Canadian reformers in 1837 b) English-Canadian reformers in 1837 c) discontented Métis in 1870 and 1885?

2) Explain how each of the following factors influences your point of view towards these rebellions: religion, occupation, education, wealth, ethnic background, political beliefs.

3) There are many important terms and concepts introduced in this account of rebellions in Canada. Can you explain the meaning of the following: rebellion, revolution, monarchy, republic, nationalism, regionalism, democracy, communism, methodism, catholicism, Orange Order, reformer, missionary, provisional government.

the rest would collapse. Middleton knew that most Indians were waiting to see who won. To white settlers, newspaper reporters and politicians, the plan ignored all the nameless terrors bred by the legends of Indian wars. Ottawa insisted. Middleton must split his army and send Colonel Otter to rescue the frightened whites at Battleford. On April 17, Middleton reached Clark's Crossing on the South Saskatchewan. Soon, his little army numbered eight hundred men. Perhaps he could still split his force and attack Batoche from both sides of the river. Using an old ferry, he transferred half his men to the far bank and set off again on April 23.

Where were the Métis? If they had not attacked Middleton's untrained soldiers, it was not Dumont's fault. Riel had refused to allow it, saying that it would be too barbaric. For weeks, the Exovedate met, listened while Riel prayed and solemnly debated whether hell was eternal. At last, Dumont's patience broke. Whether Riel liked it or not, he would attack.

On the evening of April 23, Dumont started south. By the time he reached Fish Creek, he had counted only 150 Métis and Indians, too few for a night attack. Instead, he put his men in a steep gully running across Middleton's route. When the Canadians marched into the narrow valley, he would trap them like buffalo.

Middleton was too experienced a soldier to be caught like that. His scouts, commanded by the same Major Boulton who had nearly died in 1870, were well out in front. It was the Métis, not the Canadians, who were surprised. However, Dumont's men were in a strong position. As the Canadians rushed to the edge of the coulee, they were outlined against the sky and easy targets for Dumont. Attempts to rush down the bank ended in death. The screams of wounded soldiers made Middleton's men nervous. Walking among them, the old general realized how dangerous it was to go to war with raw, amateur soldiers. So did Dumont. By the afternoon, the Métis leader discovered that he was almost alone—the rest of his followers had fled.

At nightfall, Middleton pulled his men back and made camp. Rain had turned to snow. Next day, the Canadians hardly stirred.

Selected Further Reading

LOWER CANADA

Godsell, Patricia, ed. *The Diary of Jane Ellice*, Toronto: Oberon Press, 1975. A British gentlewoman's reactions to life in Lower Canada during the rebellion and her experiences as a rebel hostage.

Schull, Joseph. *Rebellion: The Rising in French Canada, 1837*. Toronto: Macmillan, 1971. An account of the discontent.

UPPER CANADA

Flint, David. *William Lyon Mackenzie: Rebel Against Authority*. Toronto: Oxford, 1971. A biography of the volatile politician.

Kilbourn, William. *The Firebrand: William Lyon Mackenzie and Rebellion in Upper Canada*. Toronto: Clarke, Irwin, 1964. An award winning biography.

Reaney, James. *The Boy with an Я in his Hand*. Toronto: Macmillan, 1965. Through the eyes of two young boys, the Family Compact and the events prior to the rebellion are seen.

Turner, D. Harold. *To Hang a Rebel*. Toronto: Gage, 1977. A historical novel of the period.

RIEL REBELLIONS

Bowsfield, Hartwell. *Louis Riel, the Rebel and the Hero*. Toronto: Oxford, 1971. A historical account of Riel and his times.

Howard, Richard. *Riel*. Toronto: Clarke, Irwin, 1967. A Jackdaw of newspaper facsimiles, proclamations and pictures.

McCourt, Edward. *Revolt in the West*. Toronto: Macmillan, 1958. A historical account of the Riel Rebellion.

McNamee, James. *Them Damn Canadians Hanged Louis Riel!* Toronto: Macmillan, 1971. A boy and his uncle visit the West during the Riel Rebellion.

Morton, Desmond. *The Last War Drum*. Toronto: Hakkert, 1972. A study of the second Riel Rebellion.

Truss, Jan. *A Very Small Rebellion*. Edmonton: LeBel, 1977. A "revolt" led by two Métis boys parallels a factual account of the Riel Rebellion.

Index

30,819